The Blue Butterfly

Selected Writings 3: The Balkan Trilogy, Part 1

RICHARD BERENGARTEN was born in London in 1943, into a family of musicians. He has lived in Italy, Greece, the USA and former Yugoslavia. His perspectives as a poet combine English, French, Mediterranean, Jewish, Slavic, American and Oriental influences.

Under the name RICHARD BURNS, he has published more than 25 books. In the 1970s, he founded and ran the international Cambridge Poetry Festival. He has received the Eric Gregory Award, the Wingate-Jewish Quarterly Award for Poetry, the Keats Poetry Prize, the Yeats Club Prize, the international Morava Charter Poetry Prize and the Great Lesson Award (Serbia). He has been Writer-in-Residence at the international Eliot-Dante Colloquium in Florence, Arts Council Writer-in-Residence at the Victoria Centre in Gravesend, Royal Literary Fund Fellow at Newnham College, Cambridge, and a Royal Literary Fund Project Fellow. He has been Visiting Associate Professor at the University of Notre Dame and British Council Lecturer in Belgrade, first at the Centre for Foreign Languages and then at the Philological Faculty. He is currently a Bye-Fellow at Downing College, Cambridge, and Praeceptor at Corpus Christi College, Cambridge. His poems have been translated into more than 90 languages.

By Richard Berengarten

THE SELECTED WRITINGS OF RICHARD BERENGARTEN
Vol. 1   *For the Living: Selected Longer Poems, 1965–2000*
Vol. 2   *The Manager*
Vol. 3   *The Blue Butterfly*   (Part 1, *The Balkan Trilogy*)
Vol. 4   *In a Time of Drought* (Part 2, *The Balkan Trilogy*)
Vol. 5   *Under Balkan Light*   (Part 3, *The Balkan Trilogy*)

POETRY (WRITTEN AS RICHARD BURNS)
The Easter Rising 1967
The Return of Lazarus
Double Flute
Avebury
Inhabitable Space
Angels
Some Poems, Illuminated by Frances Richards
Learning to Talk
Tree
Roots/Routes
Black Light
Half of Nowhere
Croft Woods
Against Perfection
Book With No Back Cover
Manual: the first 20
Holding the Darkness (Manual: the second 20)

AS EDITOR
An Octave for Octavio Paz
Ceri Richards: Drawings to Poems by Dylan Thomas
Rivers of Life
In Visible Ink: Selected Poems, Roberto Sanesi 1955–1979
Homage to Mandelstam
Out of Yugoslavia
For Angus
The Perfect Order: Selected Poems, Nasos Vayenas, 1974–2010

To Lulu

The Blue Butterfly

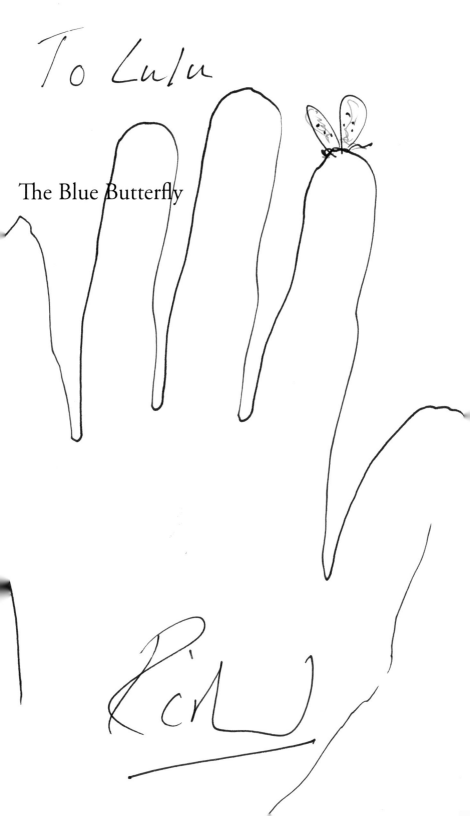

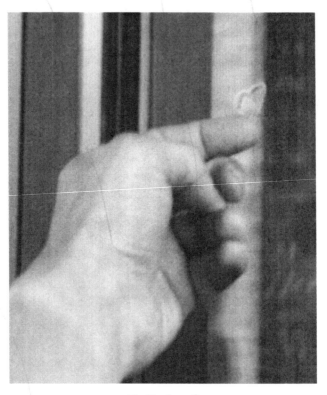

The blue butterfly
Šumarice, May 25, 1985

The Blue Butterfly

SELECTED WRITINGS
Volume 3
The Balkan Trilogy : Part 1

RICHARD BERENGARTEN

Shearsman Books

This edition published in the United Kingdom in 2011
by Shearsman Books Ltd
58 Velwell Road
Exeter
EX4 4LD

ISBN 978 1 84861 177 1

First published in paperback, 2006, by Salt Publishing, Cambridge
Second, revised edition, published in hardcover by
Salt Publishing, 2008.
This third edition, first published in 2011, contains some
textual corrections.

For the living

This story is not being told in order to describe massacres.

PRIMO LEVI
If Not Now When?

'In Yugoslavia,' suggested my husband smiling, 'everybody is happy.' 'No, no,' I said, 'not at all, but.' The thing I wanted to tell him could not be told, however, because it was manifold and nothing like what one is accustomed to communicate by words. I stumbled on. 'Really, we are not as rich in the West as we think we are. Or, rather, there is as much we have not got which the people in the Balkans have got in quantity. To look at them you would think they had got nothing at all. But if these imbeciles here had not spoiled this embroidery you would see that whoever did it had more than we have.'

REBECCA WEST
Black Lamb and Grey Falcon

Once I dreamed I was a butterfly. Fluttering around, I was completely involved in being a butterfly and was unaware of being a man. Then, suddenly, I woke up and found myself myself again. Now I don't know whether I was a man dreaming I was a butterfly, or whether I'm a butterfly dreaming I'm a man.

ZHUANG ZHOU

Contents

Illustrations

Editorial Note

The Blue Butterfly is the third of five volumes published in 2008 in the ongoing series of Richard Berengarten's *Selected Writings*. It is also the first part of his *Balkan Trilogy*, followed by *In a Time of Drought* and *Under Balkan Light*. The book's twin points of departure are a massacre that took place in Šumarice, outside the town of Kragujevac in October 1941, and an encounter with a blue butterfly at the same location in May 1985. The poems are laced into their contexts by documents, photographs, a postscript, and endnotes which provide references and dates and places of composition. In October 2007, the author received a special honour at the annual commemoration of the Kragujevac massacre, when *The Blue Butterfly* provided the theme for the oratorio at the open-air memorial event for the victims. The first publication of this book appeared in 2006 under the name Richard Burns. For the revised subsequent editions, the poet has repossessed his ancestral name.

Acknowledgements

Thanks to the editors who have previously published the following poems:

'Stagnation', *Book With No Back Cover*, David Paul, London, 2001. 'Two documents', *The London Magazine*, Feb–March, 2006. 'The blue butterfly', *The Jewish Quarterly*, London, Nº 148, London, Winter 1992–3; *Against Perfection*, King of Hearts, Norwich, 1999; *Passionate Renewal: Jewish Poetry in Britain since 1945*, Five Leaves, Nottingham, 2001; and *Poetry at Porto Santo: Que paz dessas guerras?* Governo Regional de Madeira, Portugal, 2004. 'Nada: hope or nothing', 'The death of children', 'There is scant hope', 'Traces we cannot name' and 'Nothing is lost always', *Against Perfection*, King of Hearts, Norwich, 1999. 'Clean out the house', *The Jewish Quarterly*, London, Nº 148, London, Winter 1992–3, and *Against Perfection*, King of Hearts, Norwich, 1999. 'There is no comfort', 'Fifth wreath', 'Sixth wreath' and 'Seventh wreath', *The Liberal*, October–November, London, 2006. 'War again: Yugoslavia 1991', *Out of Yugoslavia, North Dakota Quarterly*, Vol. 61, Nº 1, Grand Forks, Winter 1993. 'Ballad of the seagull: the schoolboy', *For the Living*, Salt, Cambridge, 1st edition, 2004. 'Unmarked voices from a mass grave', *Tel Aviv Review*, Winter 1989. 'This country weighs so heavy', *Tel Aviv Review*, Winter 1989; *Klaonica*, Bloodaxe Books, Newcastle upon Tyne, 1993; and *Out of Yugoslavia, North Dakota Quarterly*, Vol. 61, Nº 1, Grand Forks, Winter 1993. 'The untouchables', *Tel Aviv Review*, Winter 1989; *Celtic Dawn* Nº 5, Thame, 1990; prize in Yeats Club annual competition; and *The Jewish Chronicle Literary Supplement*, London, 11 January 1991. 'Wayside shrine', *Scintilla* No 7, The Usk Valley Vaughan Association, Llantrisant, 2003; and *For the*

Living, Salt, Cambridge, 1st edition, 2004. 'The dead do not hear us', *Shearsman*, Exeter, N⁰ 59, Summer 2004; http://www.shearsman. com. 'What power or intelligence', *Shearsman*, Exeter, Nos 67/68, Spring 2006. 'True to your absence, glory', *Chorus*, N⁰ 2, Genova, December 2004; and *Los Poetry Press* poem cards, Cambridge, December 2005. 'Don't send bread tomorrow', 'When night covered Europe', 'A twentieth century dream' and 'Conversation between a butterfly and a murdered man at one of the entrances to the Underworld', *Great Works*, Issue 6, Summer 2006; http:// www.greatworks.org.uk. 'The conquerors" and 'In silence: the mourner', *Tremblestone*, Plymouth, August, 2006. The conquerors', 'In silence: the mourner' and 'The corners of the mouth', *Shearsman*, Exeter, Nos 69/70, Autumn 2006; http://www.shearsman.com. 'Shalom', *Los Poetry Press* poem cards, Cambridge, December 2005, and *Great Works*, Issue 6, Summer 2006; http://www.greatworks. org.uk. 'Grace', *The Jewish Chronicle Literary Supplement*, London, 11 January 1991; *Los Poetry Press* poem cards, Cambridge, December 2000; and *Book With No Back Cover*, David Paul, London, 2001.

For their valuable comments and suggestions during the final editing of this book, I should like to thank Melanie Rein, Anthony Rudolf, Anthony Davies, Philip Kuhn and Joanne Limburg. Thanks also to: the early translators of some of these poems into Serbo-Croat, Bogdana G. Bobić, Hanifa Da Lipi, Moma Dimić, Ivan Gadjanski, Danilo Kiš, Ivan V. Lalić and Daša Marić; the poet and broadcaster Duška Vrhovac, who made a documentary programme for Yugoslav national television based on the title poem; the entomologist Isidor Šarić, who gave advice on butterfly identification; and Yakovos Kampanellis, who kindly gave his permission to include versions of his poems, 'Όταν τελειώσει ο πόλεμος' ('When this war is over') and 'Ο δραπέτης' ('Man on the Run'). I am particularly grateful to Vera V. Radojević, the translator of this book into Serbian, for her patient help in research and in translating documents and correspondence. For some of the information in the Postscript, and for bringing me up to date with the latest research on the Šumarice massacre, I am indebted to the Kragujevac writer Slobodan Pavičević and to the historian Staniša Brkić, Head of the 21st October Memorial Museum at Šumarice, both of whom have edited books and written widely on themes connected with the 1941 atrocity. Stanisa Brkić, the leading authority on the Kragujevac massacre, has not only generously supplied me with documents and photographs but has also kindly allowed me to quote from a hitherto unpublished monograph of his.[1]

For other forms of help, criticism and encouragement, I should also like to thank Ratko Adamović, Gully Burns, Lara Burns, Predrag Bogdanovic Ci, Ned Goy, Zlatko Krasni, Vesna Kovačević, Kim Landers, Jasna Levinger-Goy, Rade Jovetić, Peter Mansfield, Ivana Milankova, Jasna B. Mišić, Arijana Mišić-Burns, Rosemary Musgrave, Dimitrije Nikolajević, Nataša Nikolajević, Branka Panić, Aleksandar Petrov, Adam Puslojić, Aleksandra Radojević, Slobodan Rakitić, Radoslav Tilger and Jelena Vojvodić. For permission to publish the photographs of the Kragujevac mass arrests and massacre, and the last messages of victims, thanks to the Director of the 21st October Memorial Park at Šumarice, Vladimir Jagličić; and for permission to publish the photograph of Stjepan Filipović on the gallows, thanks to Vladimir Krivošejev, Director of the National Museum, Valjevo.

Finally, my special gratitude to friends who have died since this book was conceived: writers, poets, translators and scholars, who generously gave me their time, attention, humour, affection and hospitality, and, in varying ways, influenced the writing of *The Blue Butterfly*: Bogdana G. Bobić, Oskar Davičo, Edward D. Goy, Jovan Hristić, Svetozar M. Ignjačević, Bernard Johnstone, Danilo Kiš, Ivan V. Lalić, Desanka Maksimović, Vasko Popa, Peter Russell and Eugen Werber. May this book offer a kind and loving tribute to their memory.

All interpretations and opinions expressed in this book are, of course, my own.

RB
CAMBRIDGE
APRIL 27, 2006

---

[1] Added for the 2nd edition, 2008: Stanisa Brkić's monograph, entitled *Ime i broj: Kragujevačka tragedija 1941* ['*Number and Name: The Kragujevac Tragedy 1941*'] was published in 2007 by Spomen-Park Kragujevački oktobar ['The Kragujevac October Memorial Park'], Kragujevac.

1 The blue butterfly

Stagnation

Skies slept, or looked
the other way.
Exonerate nobody.

The eye-of-heaven's
retina detached.
Justice cataracted.

On earth, men
slaughtered, fell
and rotted.

And the dead
and living dead
sank deeper in decay.

Darkness flowered
in cruelty. Gracelessness
numbed hope.

Heaven there, world
here, and their only
meeting place, death.

Two documents

In Serbia, due to the Balkan mentality, widespread
communism, and patriotically camouflaged uprisings
it is necessary that the orders of the High Command
be carried out with extreme severity. The quick
and ruthless suppression of the Serbian uprising

represents a considerable gain towards the final
German Victory, which must not be underestimated.
In the event of loss of German soldiers' lives
or the lives of the Volksdeutschers, the Local
Commanders and, ultimately, the Regimental Commanders

will order immediate executions of the enemy
according to the following guidelines: a) for each
murdered German soldier or Volksdeutscher
(man, woman or child) 100 prisoners or hostages;
b) for each wounded German soldier or Volksdeutscher

50 prisoners or hostages. All of Serbia must become
a terrifying example which will strike at the hearts
of the people. Each man who behaves kindly
sins against his dead friends and regardless of rank
will be held responsible before the Court Martial.

Report, October 30, 1941

The severe attacks by the Wehrmacht, especially
    the ruthlessly executed reprisal measures
seemed to have led to a sobering up
    of at least part of the Serbian population
by the end of October. According to a report
    of 30.10.41 of the Plenipotentiary
Commanding General in Serbia, a total
    of 3,843 Serbs were arrested. In Belgrade
405 hostages were shot (until now a total
    of 4,750), 90 Communists in Šabac,
2,300 hostages in Kragujevac, and 1,700
    in Kraljevo. The prison camp
at Šabac on October 15 contained 19,545
    Serbs. Bands also had to be driven
from their hide-outs in the mountains
    and woods south of Kragujevac.

Don't send bread tomorrow

October 21, 1941–May 25, 1985

Marched out of town, herded in huts and barracks,
from workshops, factories, offices, prisons,
classrooms, living rooms, and off the city's streets,
they heard shots outside, knew their own deaths near,
and on scraps of paper emptied from pockets
scribbled quick messages to loved ones.

> *Dad – me and Miša are in the old barracks*
> *Bring us lunch, my jumper too and a rug*
> *Bring jam in a small jar*
> *Dad see the Headmaster if it's worth it*
> *I'm OK how are things at the mill*
> *As for that raki great you've sent it*

Carpenter, tavern keeper, cobbler, clerk,
locksmith, gunsmith, foundry worker, priest,
the teacher who refused a collaborator's rescue
but chose instead to step out to his death
with the schoolboys he taught, calling
Go ahead. Shoot. I am giving my lesson. Now.

> *Tell the comrades to fight till they crush the enemy*
> *I'm done for but let them wipe out the vermin*
> *My darling wife maybe we shall never meet again*
> *Write to my mother tell her everything*
> *For the sake of whatever's dearest to you revenge me*
> *Children revenge your father Stevan*

And forty-four years later, a young father carries
his toddler on his shoulders, chubby arms waving,
carefully around a flower bed, hoists the child
to perch astride their grave, while he crouches,
hidden behind a slab, and calls to his friend,
Go ahead. Shoot. Take a photograph. Now.

> *Tsveta goodbye take care of our children*
> *Mira kiss the children for me children listen to mum*
> *My dear sweet children your dad sends you his last words*
> *Goodbye I'm going to death may God protect you*
> *Forgive me if I offended anybody in my life*
> *Don't send bread tomorrow*

The blue butterfly

On my Jew's hand, born out of ghettos and shtetls,
raised from unmarked graves of my obliterated people
in Germany, Latvia, Lithuania, Poland, Russia,

on my hand mothered by a refugee's daughter,
first opened in blitzed London, grown big
through post-war years safe in suburban England,

on my pink, educated, ironical left hand
of a parvenu not quite British pseudo gentleman
which first learned to scrawl its untutored messages

among Latin-reading rugby-playing militarists
in an élite boarding school on Sussex's green downs
and against the cloister walls of puritan Cambridge,

on my hand weakened by anomie, on my
writing hand, now of a sudden willingly
stretched before me in Serbian spring sunlight,

on my unique living hand, trembling and troubled
by this May visitation, like a virginal
leaf new sprung on the oldest oak in Europe,

on my proud firm hand, miraculously blessed
by the two thousand eight hundred martyred
men, women and children fallen at Kragujevac,

a blue butterfly simply fell out of the sky
and settled on the forefinger
of my international bloody human hand.

Nada : hope or nothing

Like a windblown seed, not yet rooted
or petal from an impossible moonflower, shimmering,
unplucked, perfect, in a clear night sky,

like a rainbow without rain, like the invisible
hand of a god stretching out of nowhere
to shower joy brimful from Plenty's horn,

like a greeting from a child, unborn, unconceived,
like an angel, bearing a gift, a ring, a promise,
like a visitation from a twice redeemed soul,

like a silent song sung by the ghost of nobody
to an unknown, sweet and melodious instrument
buried ages in the deepest cave of being,

like a word only half heard, half remembered,
not yet fully learned, from a stranger's language,
the sad heart longs for, to unlock its deepest cells,

a blue butterfly takes my hand and writes
in invisible ink across its page of air
Nada, Elpidha, Nadezhda, Esperanza, Hoffnung.

The telling

First attempt

In that moment, I remembered nothing
but became memory. I *was* being.
And as for *before*? *Before* – a mouthing
of half-dumb shadows had been my hearing
and tunnels sculpted and drilled through fearing
the whole bolstered scope of my seeing.

Now my ears awakened in an alert
attentive and percipient listening
to scoured shells of voices, wholly prised apart
from those dead mouths, pouring their testament
onto spring wind, stirred by the instrument
of the butterfly at rest on my finger, glistening.

And I saw the May morning sun shoot fire
on the hillsides, which still glowed green, intact,
and those massed children, I heard as a choir,
although still only schoolkids, who chattered.
Nothing was marred or maimed. Everything mattered.
Matter was miracle. Miracle was fact.

As though an index to the infinite
library of nature and history
had tumbled into me, and a fortunate
finding of buried keys, of forgotten
reference and disappeared quotation
had filled my sight, as gift, as mystery,

all was ordinary, still – and, yet, otherness
without seam. The world did not sheer away
but was its very self, no more nor less
than ever, but tuned now to its own being,
and the heard and seen *were* hearing, seeing,
spirit within spiral, wave within way.

Second attempt

Nobody could stay unmoved in this place,
not blench at all, not flinch with at least some
tightening of skin, muscles of throat and face
or watering of eyes. *We who live on*
might have been them. There's no prerogative on
pain. Cruelty's commonness makes us all dumb.

Numb silence, though, is no answer to evil.
To remain tacit, to call up no speech on its
repeated occurrences, is to grovel
before it, as to some pre-ordained essence
demanding just as complete acquiescence
as the rotations of seasons and planets,

and that won't do. Fail or not, I must try
this telling: like a treadmill, mangle, wringer,
or spinning drum squeezing spongy death dry,
let me crush thought, sacrifice-soaked, to drain
oil from slaughter, juice from the fruit of pain
into my blood, along my writing finger,

channelled in flight by you, fully fledged nymph,
that their heroisms might dizzy my head,
their red corpuscles flow through my lymph
and their strength fill me, as wind fills a sail –
if only for once, words, words would not fail
ever to reach the dumb mouths of the dead –

to carry a cargo of such immense weight
of souls from the hold of their burying ground,
seal pain, refine death, transubstantiate
blood, to wine, to spirit. This, blue fritillary,
flight filtered fine in a poem's distillery,
is how I would ring their memorial sound.

Third attempt

Is it *language itself* won't do here? When time flows
into itself, and space is so transparent
there's no gap between the knower who knows
and the knowing, what sounding images break
more than faintest echoes, or scratches opaque
as mist shadows etched against the apparent?

Can one tell, or even utter, what was utterly
simple, wonderful, terrifying, total
and wordless? I want to tell – an errant blue butterfly
sat on my finger and weightlessly pressed
two thousand eight hundred souls laid to rest
in one thrust through me, and that wound was fatal.

I want to tell – there can never be going
back, failing, fading away or withdrawal
from that moment's blessing, which goes on flowing
in its entirety, wave on wave, through
and through me. I, as human, poet, Jew,
am held responsible for its renewal

here, in each line I trace. Ah, but plausible
though it may be to trust most of the time
in language, in telling, in the passable
undistorted transparencies of the word,
how shall miracle, resistant, absurd,
ring clean through the slickened varnish of rhyme?

If the complex sheen on those blue wing scales,
polarising light, could move one single voice
here, besides mine, who would mourn language fails
always to tell the hope needed to live,
to remind, to recall, to forgive and to give
revenge its new orders, grace to rejoice?

War again

Yugoslavia 1991

Watch where you walk. You think you tread on stones?
You're wrong, my friend. It is your brother's bones.

2   The death of children

The death of children

It is the death of children most offends
nature and justice. No use asking why.
What justice is, nobody comprehends.

What punishment can ever make amends?
There's no pretext, excuse or alibi.
It is the death of children most offends.

Whoever offers arguments pretends
to read fate's lines. Although we must swear by
what justice is, nobody comprehends

how destiny or chance weaves. Who defends
their motives with fair reasons tells a lie.
It is the death of children most offends.

Death can't deserve to reap such dividends
from these, who scarcely lived, their parents cry.
What justice is, nobody comprehends.

Bring comfort then, and courage. Strangers, friends,
are we not all parents when children die?
What justice is, nobody comprehends.
It is the death of children most offends.

There is no comfort

A mother

There is no comfort. What comfort can come,
when neither here below nor up on high
are love and justice more than martyrdom?

Who cares what may, or may not now become
of me, whom nothing new can horrify?
There is no comfort. What comfort can come

now my whole joy is gone? How wearisome
that nowhere in this world, until I die,
are love and justice more than martyrdom.

Tell me in truth if you can offer some
crumb of real hope to me from earth or sky.
There is no comfort. What comfort can come

from graveyard or from crematorium
to one like me, with no tears left to dry?
Are love and justice more than martyrdom?

I stand in accusation, though I'm dumb
with grief, and can't speak any more. Why try?
There is no comfort. What comfort can come?
Are love and justice more than martyrdom?

Bloody in vengeance

A father

Bloody in vengeance, red in tooth and claw,
devouring beauty, innocence and youth,
snarling at human longing, love and law,

in sickness, drought, plague, sacrifice, rape, war,
most keen and spry, in loathing nothing loath,
bloody in vengeance, red in tooth and claw,

slave to the pimp of fate, his favourite whore,
pump of delusions, sworn on sacred oath,
snarling at human longing, love and law,

ally of flies, rats, jackals, drooling jaw
monstrously cunning, cruel, coarse, uncouth,
bloody in vengeance, red in tooth and claw,

with ever greedy belly, ready maw
gaping, spitting and belching, a foul mouth
snarling at human longing, love and law,

Nature slinks onward. Ask me no further, for
this is the truth and nothing but the truth,
bloody in vengeance, red in tooth and claw,
snarling at human longing, love and law.

A hollow dream

A mother

But now her birth is like a hollow dream.
Since she is nowhere, nothing, gone for good,
my womb contracts, a huge and empty scream.

The common miracle, a normal theme
taken for granted, that was motherhood.
But now her birth is like a hollow dream.

Hope had a pattern once. Joy had a scheme
I wrongly thought I'd fully understood.
My womb contracts, a huge and empty scream.

Other than this, who knows what more extreme
pains, even tortures, I could have withstood,
but now her birth is like a hollow dream.

This is a pain without stitch, hem or seam,
a coffin shroud, drum-tight as hardened wood.
My womb contracts, a huge and empty scream.

This voice of mine's too vacant to blaspheme,
but I would curse Creation, if I could,
for, now her birth is like a hollow dream,
my womb contracts, a huge and empty scream.

Something more?

A father

To ask what I was made a human for,
I've intellect and conscience. But for this?
This suffering? Isn't there something more?

That seagull on the wind, there, see him soar
on his wide arc. But I have consciousness
to ask what I was made a human for.

Everything I have built here to endure
lies ruined now, a crumbling edifice.
This suffering? Isn't there something more?

If I could fly through heaven's gate, as sure
as that white bird, across the sea's abyss,
to ask what I was made a human for,

I'd scan and scour time backwards for a cure
for this bereavement, to our genesis.
This suffering? Isn't there something more?

But here I stand, in ignorance, at death's door,
quite terrified, as on a precipice,
to ask what I was made a human for.
This suffering? Isn't there something more?

There is scant hope

There is scant hope. Yet courage still there is
to thread love through the fibres of the tree
that outspans and outlasts our histories,

and though we go the ways of twigs and berries,
branches and leaves, and in mortality
there is scant hope, yet courage still there is,

and there's no choice but love. There never is,
through miracle or through catastrophe
that outspans and outlasts our histories.

So we must love, despite life's treacheries,
time's wastefulness, death's crass absurdity.
There is scant hope. Yet courage still there is

to love again. Life through our arteries
drives love, the soul's first, purest quality
that outspans and outlasts our histories.

The lines of chance and fate are mysteries
we comprehend best when we clearly see
there is scant hope. Yet courage still there is
that outspans and outlasts. Our history's.

Clean out the house

Clean out the house for springtime. Sweep the floor
in patience and in conscientiousness.
Let in the wind that's hammering at the door.

Who knows, some day we'll hammer out a cure
for cruelty, corruption, cowardice,
clean out the house for springtime, sweep the floor,

create a pattern, not caricature
of natural justice, without prejudice,
let in the wind that's hammering at the door.

But human suffering? Don't be so sure.
In practice every theory goes amiss.
Clean out the house for springtime. Sweep the floor.

We go the way the flies go. Dust, manure
or ashes will be all that's left of us.
Let in the wind that's hammering at the door.

We can trust nothing, nowhere rest secure
except in love, for love is limitless.
Clean out the house for springtime. Sweep the floor.
Let in the wind that's hammering at the door.

3 Seven wreaths

First wreath

From what remains of the Kragujevac dead,
who have become mere mineral and memory,
massed flowers, in a triumph of living red,
breed in a soil where corpses calcify.
They trumpet silent bells out of these graves
blazing against green hills and maytime sky
like purest flame-hearts. These were Slavs, not slaves,
this flower-music calls. And even though
the mind derails in horror here, and raves
awhile through nameless, frameless spaces – so
evil, I lose sense of what it feels
to have a heart that beats at all – a slow
      music of colours plays on sense and seals
      gone sounds of gunfire and of clicking heels.

Second wreath

Tulips, roses, geraniums: a year-round
plaited wreath of crimson and scarlet skeins
these valleys with a slow fugue of no sound,
staining time cochineal around war's scorns
and losses, knitting dusty webs on waste
and over deaths, like a spider. My brain scans
inwards, outwards, weaving through the worst
cacophonies of nightmare, whose plagues deafen,
stunning thought and perception in a tide
of filth no flower's scent can mask or soften.
The mental stench of soil soaked in spilt blood
drowns out even the blueness of this heaven
      and mingles on this green palette to flood
      into a trench of corpses, pooled in mud.

Third wreath

Whose is this temple? Memory's? Or Death's?
If Death were Führer of this sky's pavilion,
who could deny him, however many breaths
we yet might breathe? Three thousand here, six million
or more of my own people throughout Europe –
merely for more massed lives to pour vermilion
floods into brimful slaughter, without hope –
as effortlessly as any flower that grows,
to rot, and pour its petals down this slope,
existing to exist, then decompose?
What upward-turning silent chime of tulips
would ring more than despair, or scent of rose,
    if Death were sole-task master, rattling pips
    like husks on wind? Then I should seal my lips.

Fourth wreath

Could flowers' quiet voices avenge these fallen?
Perennially they change, their colours blow,
they open, bloom, precipitate their pollen,
they tower, wither, die. But their songs grow,
dropping their seed and breeding in their prime,
for unborn generations, for tomorrow.
Should ever judgement come to fit this crime,
should these dead but awaken, and their tombs
throw up their burdens, in that timeless time
when earth harvests redemption, then these blooms
will rise with scaly wings, like imagos
of butterflies, blue heralds, cloudy grooms,
      for which, weak angels, harbingers, time shows
      you now, on earth, in blood and crimson rose.

Fifth wreath

Music of reds and crimsons, battle on.
Continue calling out until the seven
thousand men and boys slaughtered like cattle on
this green hill, in crass insult to blue heaven,
breed children's children's children, to change all
to change revenge: until revenge is even
against revenge. Sing on, until revenge'll
take vengeance on itself, take eye for eye
no more: until each flower becomes an angel –
no longer seeding, breeding here to die
in dignified remembrance, apt memorial,
bleeding into these Balkan hills and sky –
     and do not seal your silent lips until
     red stands for more than their avenging will.

Sixth wreath

Against revenge? No. Just a mass of flowers.
While destinies lie mapped in spiral ways'
unfathomable mazes, and our hours
of waiting for true justice stretch to days,
centuries turn to aeons, and more pain,
cruelty, cunning, cowardice, outweigh praise,
and being is unrealised, hope vain,
history a legend without a moral,
dull habit, our becoming, endless drain
of expectation, lit up by ephemeral
delicate perfumed glimpses flowers bring –
these papery rubies strewn on beds of emerald
in pliable quilts of yet another spring
reveal no answer. But they sing. They sing.

Seventh wreath

Blue butterfly, with blood sewn in your hem,
your pattern carries, and is copied through
an unseen thread that shimmers in each stem
to bloom again, variegated, new,
from every bulb that flowers on this heath
where blood and spirit make their rendezvous.
Crowning earth men and children sleep beneath,
grass tops their graves. Flowers are their diadem,
weaving their petals in a living wreath
spun, unseen, from the soil heaped over them,
perfuming this entire necropolis
and bugling to the wind their requiem.
     Rooted in death, but death's antithesis,
     what is this wreath, if not hope's chrysalis?

4 Seven songs of the dead

The shadow well

Stand up, Soldier, ring the bell,
ring it for yourself as well.
Sentry, shut your telescope,
surrender your horizon's hope.

Climb up, Deacon, to the tower,
pull the rope and ring the bell.
The butterfly burns on its flower.
Gunner, you will die as well.

Ask the bloody Brigadier
why I shat myself in fear
but never emptied out the bucket
and just told him to go fuck it.

And ask the ribboned Generals
talking in luxurious halls
if they tremble where they sit
while I rot in a common pit.

Survivor, go ask Presidents
Does this sacrifice makes sense?
And will the international liars
negotiate to quench these fires?

Around this blaze, fierce shadows grope
inward to quench any hope.
Pull the rope, ring the bell
What else is there left to tell?

Pull the rope, ring the bell,
wind blows in an empty shell.
Like a flickering from hell
light flecks in the shadow well.

When night covered Europe

Second song of the dead

You who pass this way
in European day
know who walked among
these hills and valleys
a man and a boy
with nothing to say
but half-remembered poems
carrying a machine gun
when night covered Europe

In a mountain village
a woman gave them porridge
and space by her fire
cornmeal and milk
crumbs rich as knowledge
kindness to mend courage
of a man and a boy
carrying a machine gun
when night covered Europe

From a hovel hidden
among rocks and boulders
a girl with smouldering eyes
ran after, calling
take me with you, soldiers
I can man a machine gun
I have two dead brothers
Now I have three others
when night covered Europe

Sleepless in bombed barns
they starved in the gloaming
but kicked over their embers
and left with no traces
to clamber higher spaces
where no armies trundle
and no dead comrades' faces
moan through broken dreaming
when night covered Europe

Ballad of the seagull

Third song of the dead : the schoolboy

So now it was my turn. I heard my angel call,
togged up like an officer. His guards stood in ranks.
Only then did I realise: that I had lived at all
was purest miracle. It was too late to give thanks.

Why, I half wondered, hadn't he called my name
like in school assembly? Why this senseless number?
It didn't matter much. It all came to the same.
Maybe he didn't know. Or just couldn't remember.

I shut my eyes tight, heard roaring waves and wind,
and saw a white gull, wheeling, high, behind a ship,
and on deck, the captain, drunk out of his mind,
a rifle in his hand. I bit my lower lip.

Reeling, he took aim. Light flashed from the barrel.
The seagull froze an instant in its wheeling arc.
'Withered is my darling, shorn of her apparel,'
a voice inside me whispered, and half my world went dark.

A whirring in the head. Wings around me beat
in fury as I spotted a red stain on the waves.
I sank down. Slow motion. I couldn't keep on my feet.
and ghostly faces grinned in greeting from their graves.

Where my gull had fallen, as in a haggard dream,
a whole ragged army, in frenzied disarray,
rose and marched on the waters, frozen eyes agleam,
appearing and vanishing, like flecks of spray.

'Ready yet?' they smiled. 'We've come to take you home.'
'Come, child,' they guffawed, 'Time now for bed,'
all the while tossing their heads on the foam,
the limitless battalions of dead and living dead.

Numb hands tried to paddle. Legs kicked out. In vain.
They closed around like seaweed, clawing, to drag me under.
I was caught like a coracle in a hurricane,
while all around me gunshots rolled out their thunder.

But as I tossed and pitched, there came a sudden lull,
a moment's total calm, that shook me from them, free.
and my failing eyes traced a solitary gull
sailing, a white sky-speck, a curve, a line, a V –

'They haven't got you yet,' a voice inside me laughed,
'but why then is this water stained so brightly red?'
'Fool,' hissed a corpse beneath me. 'Don't be bloody daft.
You're the one they aimed at. They've got you instead.'

I shrank. They squeezed closer. Now I heard no sound.
I wondered whose shoulders I sensed their fingers clutch,
and whose head they stroked. Some orphan they had found?
No loving father could have had a gentler touch.

'Away, away,' I mouthed. But now my tongue and lips
were almost glued together, swallowed by the crowd.
Then a new recruit fell onto me. Total eclipse.
Life poured out of me like rain from a thick cloud.

Was it men's screams or my seagull's voice I heard?
The wind bugling trees? Or some muffled, broken bell?
All was past recognition. But God knows, my white bird,
how I wished you freedom then, where the waves swell.

Straining to gaze upwards, I heard another burst
of gunfire wash over me, as from some distant hill.
'This piglet isn't cooked yet,' someone closer cursed.
So my world ended. My eyes rolled open, still.

From *Mauthausen*

Fourth song of the dead

1 Man on the Run

Yan is a man who cannot wait
Behind barbed wire is no place to be
     Now he's got out
     he wants to shout
I'm going to make it home now that I'm free

Lady, I crave a simple crust
an old set of clothes so I can change
     Please you must
     give me your trust
and help me over lake and mountain range

Wherever he stops to rest his head
the land is filled with plague and fear
     Voices cry Hide
     Don't go outside
There's a man on the run somewhere round here

A wolf to kill you Christian men
Is that how you imagine me?
     All I am
     is just a man
trying to get back home, to my country

In Brecht's country, what a wilderness
He's been arrested as a spy
     made to confess
     by the SS
and so he's been condemned to die

2 When this war is over

My darling with your eyes fixed wide in terror
my darling with your hands numb and frostbitten
when one day this war is over don't forget me

> *Joy of my life come out and kiss me*
> *Here in the street out in the open*
> *Here in the square let me embrace you*

My darling with your eyes fixed wide in terror
my darling with your hands numb and frostbitten
when one day this war is over don't forget me

> *Let me caress you in the quarries*
> *and hold you in the torture chamber*
> *beneath the eye of the machine gun*

My darling with your eyes fixed wide in terror
my darling with your hands numb and frostbitten
when one day this war is over don't forget me

> *I'll make love to you in the noontide*
> *in every place where Death is Führer*
> *until his shadow melts to nothing*

My darling with your eyes fixed wide in terror
my darling with your hands numb and frostbitten
when one day this war is over don't forget me

From the Greek of Yakovos Kampanellis

The conquerors

Fifth song of the dead

Everyone forges his fortune –
but destiny twists the metal
and, since the necessary
way is of fire, always,

when we are hot with desire
it smelts new alloys in us,
then, cooling, cracks us open
like eggshells, for the flights

of gold or grey winged eagles
or, like redundant casts
of statues to dead heroes
we would no longer recognise.

So we, who scoured pit and forest
carrying coal and wood
to stoke our own fevers
and seal ourselves inside them,

who set out brave to burn
and conquer, have come to this:
to know ourselves no more
than husks of futurity.

To his daughter, mourning

Sixth song of the dead

I speak in the crash of lilac
tumbling on graves like snow
in filigree ear-rings of bees
attached to lobes of roses
their bodies wriggling pendants
of burning tigers' eyes
and in a butterfly settling
an instant on a thyme spear.

I am those lightborn demons
who move in random dance
maddening your days
but when your dusk closes
and your sun fails
the black suns on my scales
guide me through mazes
unthreaded by cock-crow.

Unmarked voices from a mass grave

Seventh song of the dead

You have come to a place, not a place, where time and space halt,
where the trees' topmost branches stop, and the last waves stop,
and roots can grow no longer, and rivers no longer flow,
and the last heard note grips silence and never reaches further,
like a photograph of an arrow that freezes it forever
suspended in its flight, trapped quivering on air
and the moth or fly is caught in a honeyball of amber.

You have come to a place, not a place, where no-one can remember
any words they may have heard, or ways out of the maze,
or steps once learned in dancing, or their subtle variations,
and time is a catacomb, a grove of bones, a permanence,
a station and a destiny, but not a destination,
where all contours of yesterdays are stratified in a fault
and tomorrow is an abyss, and the trains of space-time halt.

5   Seven statements of survivors

This country weighs so heavy

First statement of a survivor

This country weighs so heavy
sometimes I can't breathe
Under each rock, a skull
Under the plough, teeth
In every village graveyard
names of slaughtered brothers
who fell against each other
till fish in lakes and sea
grew fat on their corpses
and in every river, blood

How many more centuries
to ease the wails of mothers
scratched in walls of farms
and hanging from barn rafters
How long before revenge
dies in its own bath
before the clansmen forget
their enemies' grandchildren
and sharpening of knives
in long awaited ambush

And yet, hard, rugged land
merciless, wild, ravaged
you have showered beauty on me
to bandage my nightmares
nourished me, filled my palms
with your bread and salt
into my mouth poured
your wine and kisses
and, gazing through open eyes
taught me to fear nothing

The untouchables

Second statement of a survivor

Most never returned. Of those who did
few talk. There are no words. No words.
What can they say to us, whose imaginations
belong only to this world, who have never been
pushed beyond the borders of the possible?

They seem, or wish to seem, unheroic,
ordinary, unmasterly, like us. And we,
who believe in words and slip on surfaces,
may never recognise behind their reticence
lie sentences so deep they are unsayable.

Noticing, we want to salute them as heroes,
but they won't have it. Rejecting eyes
behind their eyes say, No. Honours and praises
from us can never fit them. Our attention
like a uniform, makes them uncomfortable.

We are not fools. We are not especially evil.
We understand what they suffered, we think,
we care. *So tell us*, we begin . . . What stops us?
A silence behind the silence behind their silence
assuring us they know we are corruptible?

They are apart from us. It's not our fault
or theirs, we cannot reach them, that their vision
refuses more than a corner in our tomorrows,
that eyes behind their retinas make clear
questions that lie deepest are unanswerable.

It's clarity that veils them, though, not hope.
Chosen among the chosen, blessed or cursed
because they have survived the unimaginable,
as if twice born, among the living dead,
they move among us, quietly. Untouchable.

In silence : the mourner

Third statement of a survivor

On the outskirts of the city of permanent possibility,
near the fork of two rivers, where Islam and Europe cross,
a woman sits by her father's grave. She does not believe
in God, yet to the dead human, god-huge in her head,
she ferries wordless questions. On the grave, May flowers,
she has arranged carefully, a variegated bouquet
bought from the corner kiosk near her two roomed apartment
on the eighth floor of a block on the Street of National Heroes
where she lives with her daughter from a broken marriage
and a lover who does not love her. This woman has any age
but her time is just past beauty. Among graves and flowers
she sits to escape and find herself. And the dead man
she addresses, although she knows he is nowhere,
will send her clearer answers on sudden flights of images
than any plied by the living on versatile word currents
strung sparkling, multi-faceted along well-worn thought-strings,
till a thousand and one particulars, of injustices and joys,
unjumble their tangled threads, recover weight and balance,
lightborne, freed from desire, untrammelled from memory,
onto air, like dust. And even though nothing changes
everything is changed. She knows who she is, and to be,
and, silent, takes her tram home, a woman just past beauty,
gifted with the impossible in the city of possibility,
deepened, refreshed, calmed, from talking to the dead.

Wayside shrine

Fourth statement of a survivor

I

There are no choices at crossroads
after or before. The path you chose
chose you.

Hope lies through the teeth
of necessity. The way calls
unforeclosable.

In every step the traveller
plants, the irrevocable
howls at the present.

By the wayside shrine
of each moment, each
pause is perpetual danger.

So smirks the face
on this Lady who guards
every parting of ways.

2

Virgin of the wayside,
familiar of ghosts and rainbows,

lady of trinkets and spiders' webs
behind mould-gathering silence,

hostess of moths, mosquitoes
and insects of dusks and glooms,

model dressed in fool's gold,
spurious pearls and salvations,

mistress of tasteless miracles
and desperate devotions,

hear us, we beseech you,
do not hold us up too long

whose only way through fire
Is by the way of fire.

3

It is terrible to live
        only this life
and not all others possible
conceived by love and vision
on crests of wave and flame.

It is terrible to glimpse
        unexpected in corners
of rooms, streets, mirrors
images of unattainable
alternatives disappearing.

It is terrible to be haunted
        by the too familiar
presences of dead friends
in markets, corridors, trains
etched in strangers' faces.

And it is terrible to repeat
        parting after parting
from the unforgettable.
The hardest gift to bear
is always the promise broken.

4

Whether fate hears
who cares. At least
we have come this far.
And whether we shall
pass further, who knows
whether she cares.

We ask neither
her equivocal prophecy,
nor approval, nor denial,
who have no choice
but accept
life not death as fatal.

5

Maybe in its ignorance
this place will preserve
all we have shared till here
and give it someone else,

Someone who will some day
understand everything
and neither elevate
nor vulgarise us.

Although I doubt that,
may this Madonna, fat on prayer,
witness that hereon, we bear
each other in each other.

6

Mother of the wayside
soaked in superstition,

bride of the President
of the Board of Seasons,

receptionist to the underworlds
of hidden cause and effect,

nurse of false alternatives
waiting patient on tricksters,

caryatid of our fate's
empty roof above us,

queen of contradictions,
let us pass, despite you,

since the only way out
of fire is through fire.

Traces we cannot name

Fifth statement of a survivor

The too expensive treat
and the long distance call,
beauty passed by on the street
and the pinnacle too tall
for ever hope to climb,
remind us time and time
again we aren't as good
or daring as we would
most definitely prefer
to be, or wish we were.

The banned or censored book
wrung, certainly, from pain,
or the frank sexual look
of a stranger on the train
in whose beseeching eyes
we're forced to recognise
what we've imagined as
closed or forbidden, has
for us the strongest pull,
being inaccessible.

Whatever moves and lives,
sweetest when out of reach,
throws false alternatives
on the one path we each
have no choice but to take,
unravel, then remake,
yet perfumes lost on wind
still linger in the mind
and go on taking tolls
from our trawling souls.

Our brothers have gone down,
underneath the hill
with emperor and clown
as we in our time will,
audience and spectator,
player, referee,
democrat, dictator,
shareholder, employee,
pupil and professor,
sinner and confessor.

Because our being's cone
narrows like a funnel
and each of us, alone,
must go down through the tunnel,
can even strength of kin
with all of life begin
to guide us through this maze
no bloody hope can raise
to common property
of truth or liberty?

Though kinship with the living
as datum or endeavour
and honestly forgiving
are things we should not ever
breathe or live without,
being firm enough
even for preaching about
the less substantial stuff
of fellowship with the dead
fills us with fear and dread.

Though all we desire consists
of impossibilities,
and though the dream persists
and without hope this is
a mad unholy feast
for liar, fool or priest,
and though no dream alone
built Ithaca or Zion
on the pillow of a stone,
it's still desire we lie on.

As children once we dreamed
we would live for ever
and every small trick seemed
key to some endeavour
or adventure we'd be in
as hero, heroine.
When seas blew through our shell
we knew all would be well
and all we dreamed of would
be achieved in adulthood.

Though we who breathe and live
our small time on this ground
forget but can't forgive,
still must our dead surround
us all with constant flame,
and pass out keys or clues
and prompt us with their cues,
and traces we cannot name
of memory and desire
consume us in their fire.

A twentieth century dream

Sixth statement of a survivor

On street corners dried bones of animals
and humans lay in heaps, disintegrating
without a shred of flesh to cover them.
Around the city vacant fields lay charred
and smothered in a wispy veil of ash
that breezes would not sweep, but rilled in waves,
as if a shroud around a shrivelled mummy
had shifted just a little, though no rent
showed through the frizzled but still seamless fabric.

It seemed I held a camera in my hands
and moved behind it, handling its controls
with the easy skill of an experienced driver
guiding a fast car on a motorway,
and yet we drove without a trace of friction
as though we flew or floated, weightlessly –
we being just myself and the machine
pulling me onwards of its own accord
across the panorama that unfolded
soundlessly, like a movie from an archive,
scratched and staccato, often out of focus
yet in elaborate, precise, slow motion.
And so I moved, at once screened off, protected
from what the zoom lens and its monitor
rolled out inexorably before me,
but at the same time subtly glued to it,
dwelling in clinical, cold, clear detail
on every object seen through its viewfinder.

Across this deathscape lurched a single creature
a screeching half-crazed bird, its wings torn out,
long-leggèd, following behind my vehicle,
zigzagging and careering with zany energy,
at times catching up and running parallel.

Whatever had happened here had happened quickly.
Here and there, a twisted pole or pylon,
tangled in aimless wires, perched at an angle
low in the margin of the unscrolled sky,
marring its haze with indecipherable signs.
Structures of brick and stone remained intact,
casting long, linear, angular shadows,
their walls and lintels scarcely scratched or pockmarked
by faded remnants of graffiti. Wide
windows emptied of glass hung inwards on
hinges of rusted iron and sallow alloys,
giving on spaces caringly composed
as elegant interiors embodying
privacies and hospitality. Now
handles of twisted brass and aluminium
stretched out at curious angles, as if bidding
a snickered welcome through their draughty sockets
to wafting dust-gauzes, like table-cloths,
elaborately laced and hemmed in ash,
that covered half-glimpsed fragments of smashed furniture,
broken picture frames, crockery, chipped ornaments,
discoloured plaster and cracked floors and ceilings.

Statues of national heroes on their pedestals
stood steadfast in the centres of their squares,
staring, with expressionless composure,
into the further distance, at contorted
skeletons of cars caught in mid-motion,
jettisoned absurdly on slick highways
and desert boulevards bathed in liquid light.
Palms, jacarandas, poplars and acacias
had lined these roadsides, rolling out flamboyant
borders for their traffic-flow, seven lanes
wide in each direction, into the hills
and to the ocean: now wizened and blackened
charcoal trunks. Some skeletal branches clung,
spiderly upwards, webbed on emptiness,
gesturing feeble sketchmarks at the immense
burning deserted ochre of the sky
as if their cross-hatched lines might net a sun.
Dried leather skins of giant cactuses
lay draped on rocks, in whorls and rivulets,
like stony robes on statues, solid puddles,
fossils of shiny lava, honey-marbled.

Scene after scene rolled out like this, unedited,
composed of zooms and panoramic vistas
over my city, emptied in its valley,
and no-one, nothing moved, except myself
and that monstrosity, that wingless bird,
and puffs and gusts of sullen breeze that stirred
ashes and sent tremors through jagged windows.

In the cute unsubtle manner of a dream
the whole city condensed into a blob,
a glue bubble, that lowered over me,
and I was nowhere, absolutely nowhere,
encapsulated in it, trapped inside,
blind, spitting, cursing, and in fury howling.
Then the bubble, as if with a weird logic
and purpose of its own, unfathomable,
hollowed itself, with me inside it, out
and, self-detaching, in a new embodiment,
turned into that same tortured wingless bird
and flew down, first to perch on my right shoulder
and then hop, clucking, minuscule, pathetic
into my open hands, as if contented. In
the still pool of my palms I watched it shrink
and, why, I don't know, but I blew on it.
Then, shuddering as it shrivelled, in a wisp
of wind, a pressured clasp of smoke, a fleck
of sun-specked dust, a dazzling glint of flame,
it spiralled into nothingness, was gone,
leaving me only with these puppet images
I had recorded, and now send out here
in all directions, calling *Hello Hello
Come in, whoever, if you only would*

Diagonal

Seventh statement of a survivor

I met her in the shade of early evening
    in a place I did not know, and yet recalled,
    before the sun had dipped his head for crowning,

but still poured liquid light across the bay,
    when the day paused, and sniffed, before night's awning
    had opened, to let it nose its lazy way,

wagging its tail, to sleep and deep contentment.
    Her shadow, long like a tree's, I saw first, sway
    over my dusty path before the escarpment

began to level out in olive groves,
    where mountain met with sea in an embankment
    of sudden vertical cliffs above the waves.

I could not see her face, but she was beautiful.
    That silhouetted body might stir love's
    unrealised longings in me, yet be bearable,

while her hair, which blew about her in the breeze
    a subtle aura or veil, made her desirable
    yet screened her from desire. As though a frieze

had stepped out from the rockface, there she stood,
    more perfect than her copies in academies,
    a breathing, moving statue stone or wood

could never do full justice to, whose robes
    hung on the form they hid, as if a flood
    fell in a waterfall down her, and the globes

of full breasts emphasised, hid again,
  then transformed back to elemental orbs
  of jutting rock worn smooth and round by rain

or, like stones in the shallows of a stream,
  notches in the current of its water-grain.
  And now, as if she knew my self-esteem

had sunk so deep, I had lost hope, and will,
  and stood there frozen, though spring reigned supreme
  and it was May, and wild flowers on that hill

blazed their unbearable sweetness on the air,
  she turned her face towards me with a smile,
  one hand held back the sea breeze from her hair,

and the other waved and beckoned me to grope
  diagonally towards her. My despair
  turned in the wind a little up that slope

and into some small glimmer of awareness
  that hope was possible still, though not yet hope
  in that stark light, where distance all seemed nearness.

'Who are you, Lady?' I asked. And, smiling, she:
  'Whoever I may be brings you no menace.
  Therefore, come close, and listen carefully:

Time now, I must escort you to the place
  appointed you, to which you hold the key,
  though you shall never know, till sudden grace

shall light it to you in the core of darkness
    among the deepest terrors you must face
    naïvely, innocently, and in meekness,

alone, devoid of help from other men,
    where strength grows deeper taproots than deep weakness.'
    'Lady, what are you? Please?' I spoke again

so terrified, the hairs stood on my arms,
    though it was warm still, and the evening sun
    seemed not to move but, poised on its own flames,

refused to sink or blend with the horizon.
    And still she smiled. 'I have unnumbered forms,
    a name and shape for each new year and season,

according to who speaks, whose tongue, what shore,
    and all are elemental, and some, poison.
    As for you, call me keeper of that door

locked fast below fear's last extremity.
    But come. At this first meeting to say more
    builds yet more fear on your perplexity,

which is not helpful. No time for delay.
    Trust, now. And follow closely after me.'
    She turned to go. Darkness was falling fast.

I took one last look at the peaceful bay
    shimmering in pools of gold, and my whole past
    flashed, awful, through me, and I knelt to pray

there on that hill, closing my eyes aghast,
    moaning lost love. 'Come,' she called. 'Come away.
    Your soul is summoned to the secret source of day.'

6 Flight of the imago

Nothing is lost always

First flight

Nothing is lost always. Nor do things repeat themselves
identically, like a train or bus timetable,
daily or seasonally. Each journey is different.
Last time, there you sat, embedded in whatever memory
of other interiors, of yesterday night, of childhood,
staring out of the window, probably seeing nothing,
unaware whether you woke or were still afloat on dream.
This time, look, there's a fisherman, knee-deep in a pond,
a fox, silhouetted, loping over a hill brow,
an air-tailed mallard dipping his head in a stream
or a field greening or yellowed, speckled with poppies.
And next time, who will you be, other than *another*,
drinking at the station bar with some fellow traveller,
swapping jokes and anecdotes, gossiping and laughing,
or swilling alone, inside your own reflection?

When the face you know or believe you know best
changes imperceptibly each time you examine it
curiously, in the mirror, why your discomfort,
and if not curious, why did you look at all?
If, now and then, time moves like an indifferent clock,
it is not so always. Time too changes time. One day
is a rich chaos unlike any other, the sun never rises
in quite the same place as yesterday or tomorrow,
Earth deviates on its axis, pulled by vanishing stars,
the carpet of galaxies moves away under your feet
while you still stand upon it – and the one face of the other
you love, and will love always, is always the other face
of the only one you love. And that face too changes
even as you gaze. Time too changes time, like a face,
from flatness to dimension, haze to definition,
indifference to difference, humanity, height, depth – soul.

And as a surface changes to a face, unique, known, loved,
although wholly other, always wholly other,
and as a loved face may be entered, understood and known,
even if, when it happens, you cannot quite believe it,
so time's innermost fountain renews itself, murmuring,
splashing you with its language of hidden glyphs and icons,
music of impossibilities, constantly calling: 'Listen,
take me in, drink me,' and sometimes entering you too,
spreading drops on your hands, feeding your mouth with words,
unclasping your throat in song's affirmation and harmony,
like a blue butterfly. And the river of sound it forms,
flowing one way, always, then back on itself, then on,
is incapable of revealing anything more or other
than *this, this, this*. Nothing is lost always.
so learn from the clock-face, patience, until the flood
may be dived in, or gather you up like a whirlpool,
eradicating time. Memory, my treasure, only this you ensure,
darling I keep losing and finding again in the loss,
in cloud, evening, sunset, light flecks on water,
the solitary magpie's winged arc across an entire sky,
leaves, animal eyes, in whatever is closest to death,
for which, in paying nothing, we pay all we have and are –
even when you deceive, and always as miraculous
whenever you arrive, as this butterfly on my hand
and its sounding of dead voices I do not understand
how I understand. What, then, is love, but quality
of attention to details, to surfaces, and tracing
in them the depths you may call understanding
of history, which moving ever forwards, curls and coils
back on itself, as serpentine, graceful, merciless,
resisting interpretation, and losing nothing always
as the flight of this imago, time changing time?

The future recoils

Second flight

The future recoils as you approach to catch it. Glory gets
glimpsed, if at all, in heraldings and afterglows. The blue
butterfly disappears in the twinkling behind an eyeblink.

Like children playing tag with unalienable shadows
in an afternoon park or garden, or racing at break
in the playground, stopping to count to a hundred,
or turning and turning till dizzy, then opening eyes
and stretching shaky arms to find themselves,
although still themselves, in a different dimension
where, in passing, they cannot fail to cross paths
with perfection, and cannot fail to make that crossing
now, not on tomorrow's far side, sliding, like Alice,
imperceptibly through some invisible screen
in an effortless slippage across time's barriers,

occasionally we too sense we reach right through
time's surfaces or contours, even if not to its core,
and the edges of our voices suddenly stretch out
to reach and touch notes, albeit quavering, faltering,
they've never been capable even of approaching before.

See, slithering down a bank onto a path to a glade
or hiding between embankments out of sight of houses
to make secret pacts with angels, again and again
come the children. And though there is no belonging
to anything for anything ever long enough, those pacts
do get made, and get kept as lifelines for lifetimes.
And more children come. Hope lights up their faces.

The dead do not hear us

Third flight

But the dead do not hear us, and we are not Orpheus. Why
was that singular man, crossing the street at that moment,
run down? And that child, though curable, taken? Why
these slaughtered innocents, and why those survivors?
The good friend, the man on the train, the woman
behind the counter, that old fellow who used to sit
whole evenings on his bar stool, smoke two packets,
down pint after pint, and never seem worse for wear,
the virgin of Lorraine or Toledo, the Jew from Vienna or Wrocław,
the schoolboy from Kragujevac, the noble Ethiopian,
the farmer outside Srebrenica, the librarian from Priština
and the shadowed chauffeur whose name nobody remembers
who drove the English princess and her Egyptian lover
to be crushed against a pillar in a concrete Parisian tunnel?

So many we remember but will forget in just a while,
so many no-one remembers, although they have just gone,
so many recently praised, now bypassed and ignored,
so many hardly noticed, even then, and now erased
and far too many in all, ever to remember,
though some were engraved in stone, entered in the logbook,
filed in temple archives or the public records office.
And why, in that manner, and at no other time? If no single
life weighs more or less than another, how is the balance
tipped, and how is the measuring made? In penuries?
Ages? Numbers? Hairs? Sufferings? Solitudes?
And what screens, ikons, imagos, flew or flashed
in or upon them? What, if they thought, did they think
in the precise act of dying? Or were they too engrossed
in backgrounds, surfaces, contingencies, irrelevant incidentals,
pain's precise details, the registration of particulars –

like most of us most of the time – an unwashed cup,
shoelace left undone, unwatered plant on a windowsill,
sunlight-painted patch in an angle of a wall –
to pause, reflect a little, consider ends or origins,
as they were taken over, out of sight and mind,
to the shore further than any of our dreams?

If dying is an art, and the only one each of us
is expert in by default, who wins the top prizes,
is awarded *Summa cum laude* by the invisible arbiters,
judges, examiners, angels, executioners
lurking in silence behind the dark side of the mirror?
In their all-seeing eyes, Lords of the Far Side,
who truly performs best, gets special commendations,
dispensations, permissions, perquisites, privileges,
scholarships, fellowships, directorships, the very highest
distinctions – oscars, knighthoods, ministries?
Shall it be the one who refuses, who does not go gentle,
or he who whispers 'Now' to his soul to go,
the sudden swift sprinter, long distance runner,
high flying champion – or piggy who stayed at home
to look after Mother or Grandpa, dig the allotment,
clean well and stairway, keep windowsills and doorstep
spick and polished for sudden arrivals of strangers?

Does the dimpled wide-eyed child with features unbruised
by incurable mismatches ticking timebombs in her blood cells
do her dying better than the stroke-bound nonagenarian
bedridden his rest of days, who has received final
notice to quit? Or the one caught stunned, off balance,
from an active career of tendering, by the backhanded
assurance of a unique short-term contract, with cancer?
Or the one who could not wait and prepared for the event
by jumping or diving in, as though death were a pool

and not a bottomless pit without rope or ladder?
Or that other who recklessly defied doctors' predictions,
soothsayers' bargaining and evidences of stargazers
and outran all of time like a sail before wind? And what
of the ones who, without any warning, got it
by knife-thrust, neck-blow, car-crash, air-crash,
flood, fire, explosion, dog-bite, wasp-sting, nettle-sting,
stray bullet from friendly fire, bullet aimed in the back
or in the back of the neck, throttling pillow or towel,
wrong diagnosis, lack or absence of medicine,
error by expert, dereliction by specialist,
remediable poverty, government-managed drought?

We are not Orpheus and the dead do not hear us, or care,
even if they could, to tell us, what all of them know, always,
that secret we shall never learn until we cannot break it,
till we have been sworn in too, eternally, to their silence,
trustworthy only once, like them, completely dissolved
from sap, charred leaves, peat, clay, charcoal, amber,
separated and crystallised into water and minerals,
and all our words forsaken: our tongues glued
to their velar vaults, and our lips stuck together
like immovable boulders, sealing up life's cave mouth.

Wherever we turn lurk the dead, waiting to surround us
with their barriers and blockades: like pillars, like monuments,
like comfortless sentinels, they spread above, below
to the edges of our gazes; like cliffs towering sheer
from mountains under oceans to Himalayan precipices
rising all around us, hemming us in among canyons.
There is no other horizon and wherever we stand
on this shore we shall never learn to cross them.

I want to say this simply but simply do not know how.
I should like to speak with conviction but am condemned
to stammering. Our actions are more or less decent,
commanded by brains neither dishonest nor infallible,
so how, when it comes to this, can we claim anything other
than scantest glimmerings, most fleeting premonitions?
We who are informed by such paucity of insights,
we who are not shamans, imams, rabbis, ministers,
we who have no certainty and possess absolutely
no greater authority bestowed or loaned from on high
and no accreditation to dispense or receive
special keys, codes, combinations, promissory notes
for plausible rescue, improbable deliverance, sudden
unexpected salvation, deserved reward or recompense
into this or that *Elysium*, *Nirvana* or *Paradiso* – how
can the likes of us claim anywhere anything more
than a handful of smoke and puff or wisp of dust?

But all I want is impossible. To hear and understand
whatever the dead may be saying, whatever it is they want
(that is, if they do want *something*), across this dividing gulf
between these gull-haunted, rock-dotted, island-strewn,
wind-hammered, rain-battered, sun-beaten
archipelagos they have already sailed, endlessly,
and we have yet to negotiate. Indeed, what I want
(that is, *everything*, and nothing less than miracle)
is by definition ungrantable by the invisible
puppet-masters and mistresses who pull the strings
of the living, and the dead – who may even *be*
the dead: for, whenever we try to examine them,
or merely delay or halt them, even just an instant
for questioning – as if through a telescope, or zoom
lens of a camera – they gaze away, detached,
seem not to notice us, chatter and go on chattering

oblivious among themselves, like flocks of nervous birds
about to migrate somewhere else, or like wholly
human foreigners, fulfilled in their own company
and utterly derisory, or regardless, of us –
fluent in their clammy languages of indecipherable
signs and shadows that are to us wholly insoluble
and may only be traced in such ideograms and glyphs
as flower forms, wind scents and bee murmurs, tickings
and clackings of cicadas against onsets of summer nights,
or, over hazy hills, among orchards, fields and gardens,
in hazardous, hieratic, dervish movements of butterflies –
steps, scales, figures I can never quite substantiate
let alone remember and, least of all, understand
no matter how I strain to catch at them before they
dissolve in mist or disappear in shadow, migrate and
separate, evolve into further forms, colours and movements,
or get blocked for good around unturnable corners.

And just as they ignore us now, so too will they turn
away at that precise instant when our destiny
we believe, is to meet them? While, one by one
and as though magnetised, inexorably we are drawn
painfully, slowly, towards our final conditions –
when our ends approach, shall we go on moving
at the same regulated, predetermined speed, like
cargoes in holds of ships or products on a conveyor belt –
or, like runners in a marathon approaching the very
last bend, offer one final spurt, prepare to throw heads
forward and arms high as we cross the finishing line
and, gloriously abandoning every one of the disciplines
that allowed us to reach it, stretch up exultant
hands, so they can lift us, cheer us in recognition
of our ultimate achievement, our arrival, as we

mingle souls among theirs, pour ourselves wholly
into them, as into a crowd of welcoming companions,

or, like water-drops from a fountain, fall back into the pool –

only to find at that precise instant time forever stops
and space wraps itself tightly into a parcel that contains
nothing but itself and shrinks and disappears altogether
from our own hands, and everything we have been vanishes
and consciousness itself of what we have been vanishes
and all we have imagined, believed, dreamed and aspired to,
even touched and reached, really consisted of nothing?

What power or intelligence

Fourth flight

What power or intelligence charts the unfathomable
channels and gulfs? What magnet stirs and draws
glaciers over mountains, lava through volcanoes,
waves over rocks and sand, sand through the clepsydra,
and, quicker than the fall of a single grain, wills or
drills through the brain of a merely fallible creature
the intention that guides the hand that pulls the wheel
a fraction this way or that, and so spills out more cruelties,
confusions, calamities, reeling across history, through
individual lives? Are destinies governed by motive?
Or by unpredictable dice-throws, spins on fortune's
roulette? And justice? Is there any? If so, confess
you cannot see or scry the hidden channels it flows
along, runnels it cuts through the palpable, or marks
it erodes on time. You cannot see or scry, let alone trace
patterning in the pattern, or even know if there is one.

Why will this pilot, winning at cards in the mess room,
survive tomorrow's mission, and why does that other
fellow in the corner, intent on his letter home, know
he will be shot down? Why has this team already
lost the day in advance, no matter how finely prepared,
and however experienced and respected their commander,
while that other band of leaderless desperadoes, whose
entire tactical manual consists of a sheaf of scribbles
bundled in a rucksack, their training a tasteless diet
on one obsessive dream, outrageously possess themselves
of all hope's panoplies, and dare to assume the swagger
of outright victors? Why does this man, who knows the ways
of petals and leaves, grains and stresses of wood, complex
territorial calls and love songs of parlous birds, gas

himself at dawn on a shuttered car's exhaust fumes
in the snowbound front garden outside his own garage?
And what lottery makes of one woman a stony faced
harridan, surly through each of her marriages,
grasping through divorces, despite all previous
generosities of privilege, rank, fortune, beauty's
adornments from birth, even parental love, yet
bequeaths this other, raised in a tenement,
not especially lovely, intelligent or gifted, such
inviolability in the radiance of her passion
that even the crassest and clumsiest of her lovers
is awed, humbled, transformed by the gift she gives –
herself – till he curls, spent and snoring, dreaming
himself a child again, as his frame rises and falls,
like a schooner moored in harbour, while she, wide
awake, smiling, lies cradling his head on her breast?

Whose are the powers that distribute the world's
talents and gifts so unequally: between the corrupt
minister, who by hiring unscrupulous managers,
will always be successful in twisting the law
to monopolise futurity, while the upright
poor citizen, steadfast in outmoded honour,
will die for his scruples rather than ask one favour
let alone tell a lie or commit one rotten deed,
although his whole family be bound to go under?
What hand, against the odds, pulled the Warsavian
musician out of the queue from ghetto to gas chamber,
denied Death his murder, and saved this man to play
for thirty more years of audiences? Why was he chosen?
Why him and not another? And why have fate's
faceless administrators selected that impoverished
aging woman, in her damp shabby apartment
stinking of tobacco smoke, for a stab in the back

from a deranged neighbour, whom she asked in
for tea and a biscuit, because she took pity on him?
How can a life depend on something so trivial?
A biscuit. And can such minuscule details determine
history's shapes? What causes, if any, cause cause?
Originary principles? Chemical switches? Spirals
of predictive genes? Are master keys to structures of
significant action to be picked out of bunched forgettings,
insignificant details, local colours and scenarios,
unnoticed backgrounds? How absurd those intrusions
made by Necessity in the guise of mere appearance
which, if ever recognised, only get disentangled
afterwards, and frequently too late, as Fate's quirk
and sleight of hand. Unstitching the threads knitted
by time into time, invisibly, isn't hard in the contoured
editings of hindsight, nor is their staining and patterning
with retrospective imperatives. Tess's letter to Angel
should never have gone unread. She did not deserve
that. Desdemona should never have dropped her lacy
handkerchief. If only (*enter name*) hadn't got up to catch
the earlier train for a meeting that September morning
scheduled at the Twin Towers. Spilt milk, spilt blood.

Yet when armed units from his region's other tribe,
led by masked mercenaries with outlandish accents,
arrived by night in trucks to raid his village, and herded
two hundred and seventeen men and boys into a barn,
what external signal, click of bolt in barrel, dawn
flicker reflected off metal, half-glimpsed between loose
planks in a fence, crunch of boot, somewhere
outside the gate, warning from on high, apparently
unconnected chill running up and down his spine
inexplicably prompted this one prisoner, an easy-going
man, never before noted by his family or workmates

for being remarkably quick, brave or cunning – unlike
his elder brother or better-schooled, richer cousin –
to move to the back and fall flat on his face
before the bullets of the firing squad squirted morning death
through the flesh of his fellow-villagers locked inside
with him? What voice told him to lie low beneath
warm bleeding corpses of neighbours and companions
and, at the very moment before the assassins barred
the double doors for the last time, and threw in
straw and petrol to torch the whole building, what
irresistible command impelled him to squeeze out
of the small back window and roll away in a ditch? And
what strength, welling from what irrepressible source,
drove him to spend seven nights tottering half-crazed
through forests and over pathless mountains,
eventually to recognise – and name and accuse – his
kinsfolk's killers? Why this man? Why not any other?

Why this beautiful athlete and that dwarf or cripple?
Why this one in a wheelchair from birth and that one
deaf, dumb, blind? Why such uneven distribution
of nature's wealths and gifts? What help is
there in knowing that, under this sun of unreason,
minutiae weave and twist unpredictable patterns
and mindless impersonal factors leave
indelible fingerprints? 'That's just the way things
are,' smiled the rainbow in his head to the terrified
torture victim. 'You can die now, if you like,' whispered
the fallen gas mask to the conscript abandoned
in No-Man's Land, hands numb with cold, 'because
you can't reach me, can you?' 'I know it's absurd and
unfair, but I'll murder you just the same,' shrugged
the vast, wind-battered, unlistening savannah

to the farmer with no water, milkless mother,
starving helpless child, orphan riddled with AIDS.

Weren't we all children once? And aren't *all*
children innocent? What plan, graph or grid
plots such hidden contours, fissures, meridians,
poles and equators of hopes and expectations,
blunt zeroes of time's beginnings, and infinitudes
of space-ends? Is there no constant, to be
grasped, clasped, clung to? Or even glimpsed
or grazed in a moment's fractal shimmerings?

The detached Goddess *Ananke* pours acid on our eyes
and smiles the far-away smile of a lover, thug
or torturer. Is it life itself that's cruel, since we must
all die anyway, or just human stupidity rips us
in shreds and kills off the innocent, and makes
questions like these imponderable, except in the flashes
that, without announcement and for no apparent reason,
beg, even order us, to *get out* of time, as if we were
fluff on wind? I wish I could hold the moment and be
held by it, just as my blue butterfly captured my hand
and just as that photograph borrowed a moment's light
to catch its imprint for always, allowing the creature
itself, wholly unharmed, to go about its business free.

Conversation between a blue butterfly and a murdered man at one of the entrances to the Underworld

Fifth Flight

Blow on this dandelion. Spread its seeds on
the wind. I'll rest in your hand while you're dying.

Do I climb on your back, minstrel? Shrink so small you'll carry me?
Or, roped, follow you down? A stairwell? A gradual tunnel?
Or into a mine-shaft, headlong? Or shall we float without gravity?

Your time of times has come. Now is the last
of your moments. Now you must pass for ever
out of time.

        How? My hand will scarcely lift to reach and pick
your little globe. I cannot stand. Can scarcely move at all.
My breath is far too weak to blow it to its seeding place.

No matter. Matter with all its dimensions
like snowflakes, will be melted down to images,
and images into the nothingness
from which they first emerged. This is your end
and borderland, the final twist that fate
will ever knot around you. Here all lines
must stop and the entire scope of your consciousness,
like a napkin of intricate fine lace,
be folded back in and upon itself.
This is finality of angles and
very last bowing out of here and there.
Haze and smoke will begin to cover everything:
filigree webs of intermeshed perceptions,
grains of cognition, threads of body's functions,

chains of longings, spores of fulfilment, will
evaporate in mist, like morning dew.

Where and when are *we then? In what dimension of time-space
can* this *be? Is this the last end-game? Emptiness without
fanfare? No single sign of greeting? Not even the simplest
dignity or ceremony? No sole mark of farewell?*

'Here' is the infinitely spanned hiatus
between not-time and time, the final pause
given you to rest for a single instant
before one of the gates, countless, unseeable,
that leads down to the Underworld, this being
your special entrance, open for you only.
In time, this was a river and a way.

*What of the river, then, with its first chilly springs, its ripples
and torrents, backwaters and rapids, clear and polluted stretches,
broadened saline estuary and reedy marshlands? What of
the path onwards?*

Onwards? That was a bell,
when act and doing both were necessary,
to wake you up each morning. But this
is something else: no *when* or *where*
or *in* or *out of which*. It is an edge,
a brink, *without-within*, one that is best
described by *notness*, by negations of
what may be defined. So in this not-here,
we pause for an immeasurable instant
in what might well be signposted as no
man's land, contested gap between time-end
and time, a pause that is never a pause.

Seeing what I know, or believe or think I know, is sparse,
and seeing the whole scope of what I do know is excelled
so vastly by not-knowing, how do I ever grasp this?

If your knowledge were an expanding sphere,
the face of its circumference would be
the edge between your knowing and not knowing.
Your areas of ignorance would measurably
spread at the exact pace of that expansion.
Now think of turning that sphere inside out.

From now on, shall my trust be formed not on what I do know,
but on what lies outside the whole circuit of my experience?

For you no onwards is possessed by now.
After-this-now does not exist, is nothing.
Outsides and insides also have no difference.
Trust was always steeped in sweltering ignorance.

You dangle me through voids like a puppet on strings of sophistries.

I do not speak in riddles or enigmas.
Language has gaps and holes and in them lurk
many incomprehensible expanses
more copious than the sum of everything
meticulously collated and catalogued
in dictionaries and encyclopaedias.
In the faulty speech current and acceptable
on this side Death, despite its hazinesses,
gulfs, lapses, shreddings, what may be said is
'Follow me, regardless of the unsayable,
I shall take you, despite what is unspeakable,
past tragic pain, and wastes of countless souls.'
Inadequate, I know. But will this serve?

Pain? Tragedy? Waste? Gross and meaningless words that insult
realities of suffering we were given no choice
to avoid, and so were crushed by, by the fatuous, appalling
accident of happening to be 'there'! Being identified
in such and such a group, and not another, by the sheer
crassness of fortune working against us, between the merciless,
weak, frightened, quivering hands of an all-too human enemy
army, hoodwinked and brutalised to believing that we were
less worthy and pure, and less noble and proud than they. Fury
still pumps adrenalin through my weakening brain and fibres.
Injustice reeks in my nostrils. I can still taste the bitterness.
We had done nothing wrong. We deserved better than that. And
so did all the miserable sufferers who went down
like me, without memorial, whom earth, fire, water closed
over, whom aftercomers will never bother to name
let alone attempt to celebrate, honour or recall.
The whole of history is filled with ghostless specks of ash
and dust, as I shall be, morsels of reploughable chemicals
useful for futurity as rich and fertile loam. For
all this shall I who am nothing now go back into nothing,
to being one entirely with the one absolute nothingness
I was in truth always part of, through which my person and
identity in this world were no more than a very brief
hiatus. Like a tear in a fabric ripped by a bullet, then stripped
from its corpse, washed and patched over again, I was no more
than a waste of space, a blip.

If these are
your last angers, last reasons, do not hold
fast onto them. For you, that chance is gone now.
Time only now to peer into your destiny,
scry what must be, accept and follow that.

Anger and uncertainty come and go. They alternate
like cowardice and bravery. But I'm past caring now.
Would you have me pretend I was never afraid of dying?

    And this, the very last of your despairs?
    In all things, everywhere, Death hides invisible.
    Every instant that specks or pocks the surfaces
    of movement takes up identical distance
    from time's unbreachable core. That span is
    zero. Think of a sphere so very minuscule
    its centre and circumference are one.

Well, minstrel, my delicate winged creature, my dream-controller,
will you take me on? I mean appoint me, take me on trust now,
away, far, into the unshapen, into the whatever-
is-yet-to-come, in which as-yet-nothing exists to hold to,
to hold on to, to be guided with or by or towards?

    Furthernesses! Futurities! Beyonds!
    Not into anywhere conceived or thought
    by spells like these, my swiftly-dying friend.
    Although it be impossible to think
    at all without them, I beg you, do, and
    do so through their notnesses! Begin now!
    My task and destiny together form
    the taking of you, not to any zone
    nor through, beyond or past any such scoping
    that may be measurable by desires, or
    retrospective wishes, for ways, paths, rivers,
    pictures of the ascending and descending
    of mountains, embarking on ocean voyages
    or final arrival in ports and harbours
    on this side. At this threshold between non-time
    and time, all such images blur and fray.

But where, my minstrel? Without space-time, how can either one
of us be, or relate, at all? And how can your fine abstract qualities be
conceived at all if not rooted and fixed in these dimensions?
You who make yourself known only when unstoppable Death calls,
tell me, where? When? Into or out of what notness do you call me?

Where but under dark. Underneath it. Under
Death. No flavour of salt hangs there, no scent
of imminent sea. No frogs croon through evening,
No fish mate in salt marshes among reeds.
No terns or gulls are glimpsed, black against skies,
or white and grey above curled, frothy waves.
No dragonflies or mosquitoes go courting
in the estuary. Here on this side, where
air buzzes with voices, each moment perches
on the edge between time and death. The brink
is here and now, always.

Now you *speak of unders and afters;*
this now, precisely, being where no-one possesses instruments
to catch and trap what will always slip between fingers like
water, or warp, twist and destroy, like fire.

In this precise
instant, ephemeral, infinitesimal,
rests a whole fortune, ready for the taking.
Do you think it could be yours? To receive it,
open palms, then, and hold them, side by side,
cupped carefully beneath it. Catch the drops!

All I wanted was impossible, even then. But anything else or less
seemed inadequate, shameful, scarcely deserving the effort
and only what was unattainable worth fighting for.

This and every moment is the entire
fortune of Fortune, whose other name is
Ananke. She was, even before time.
Whatever gifts she grudgingly metes out
and whether at any moment, you love
of detest her for her crass machinations,
were you once naïve enough to believe
she would ever let you possess what only
she controls? Allow you to enjoy it? Never!
This elder sister of Hades who hides
invisible, behind bins, trash and bushes
outside your kitchen window, peering in,
or sits, modest, beside your village well
preening herself among lizards and butterflies
and smiling her utterly detached smile,
may let you sip a little. But she knows,
as you do, you can never drink enough
and she knows your thirst is a rage, unquenchable.

But I would have had, or governed, or made, at least one thing
on this side wholly perfectly, even if small and delicate,
even if apparently insignificant and inconsequential.
I'd have left behind some mark of achievement and defiance
on the field of this war, between desire and imperfection,
to record, in passing, that I had wanted, by co-operating
harmoniously with nature, to make something of use,
a painted box, carved table, breakable pot, or to serve
clarity, through some dispassionate non-thing, like a theorem
imbued with clean elegance, or to give out, in form, colour
and perfume, an original and unexpected version of
perfection, as some new variety of rose —

                              Perfection!
But to serve whom, for what? For your own fame
and glory, as much as anyone else's.
Under this field of stars, my hopeful hopeless
friend, fellow traveller of gods and angels,
permanent death is all you may aspire to.
Death will occupy you like an invaded
territory, fallen, captured and colonised.

No matter whether poor and entirely worthless, I have
in me at least some droplets of the blood of Byron, and fire
and courage of Filipović of Opuzen and Kraljevo.
I shan't go lightly till Death completely forces me down . . .

        . . . whose name is Overlord of Riches. Think
of the mounds of corpses piled high by time
that grow taller daily, rèfuse tips so
spectacular that even death by fire
and digging out caverns deep in the earth
for secret burial, and tipping corpses
over sides of ships, can't stop their increase.
And who profits from this hoard but grim Death,
alias *Thanatos, Hades, Dis, Charon,*
plutocrat *Pluto*, brother to *Ananke*?

I know he'll steal everything, minstrel, that he'll take away
everything I have and am, which is this ephemeral present.

        Although you keep touching, fingering, grazing it,
this present you call yours remains forever
a gift unopenable, sealed hermetically.
Grasp it and it leaves in a puff of flame.
Blow on it and it is a current of air.
Catch it and it is water poured away.

Only when death perfects time is time made
perfect and its presence called irrevocable,
just as a naked statue represents
what it embodies, and is: a god. That
is why now you must go with me to death's
chill zone of shadows deep in darkness, shadows
deeper than darkness.

But, if it is only
dark there, only wholly black, how can shadows grow, since
shadows are simply stitched, sown, stretched, hemmed
borders on the interstices between darkness and light?

That is another story which belongs
to Orpheus, not you. Nature exults
in secrets, loves to hide in many veils.

That you, day's minstrel and darling, will lead me down past night,
beggars belief and logic, both of which I abandon. Let them
fall away. Now, will you take me on, out of honeyed sunlight?

You are committed anyway to going
right to the end of your end, and to bear
the weight of your foretellings.

Wait a little.
The merging of matter back into nothing wears no fear
for me. Nor this being's physical pain, which has to be
endured. But what of consciousness, identity, uniqueness?
Mine? And anybody's ephemeral human contribution?

The face of your death is always the same
distance exactly from time's core, its end.
which is also its eventless beginning.

To Death you are always naked. To you,
he is always transparent. Though apparently
in modesty he turns his head away
whenever you move, you would never notice,
precisely in that place that he vacates,
his breathless breath pursuing you relentlessly,
that entire absence of scent he exudes,
or his pocketing of emptiness from sockets
under your eyes, just as you think you see
wholly into the hearts of things themselves.
Like the sun, but a deep black one, in negative,
he won't be viewed directly without scorching
your vision out, scalpelling out your eyes.
No further consolation can be given
to your need for hope, absolute, than this.

Take me, minstrel. It is enough. To see you, is enough,
to filter away blurs and shadows that surround me, find
courage to go with a certain understanding of irony and
at least some degree of quietness, clarity, transparency.

Though I rise over deaths like the blue core
in living flames, though I step light on what
I touch, though I make future and past disappear,
my function is not discovery, still
less speech. I prefer easy paths on air
across fields and meadows, where it is good
to settle and nestle inside heads of flowers.
You pass through these gates. I protect and watch them.

Angel of life or death, my butterfly, no matter. You
blue speckler and flecker of wind, handsomest airborne drifter,
master lightfoot, with your club-tipped antennae, go, shimmering.

98

What then is singing?
And what dancing?

Sixth flight

What then is singing but an emptying and replenishing
of the full cup of memory, into now and always
from the source of always and now? When the merely human
voice is possessed of another power than gesturing or calling
to particular self or other, requiring, needing, demanding
mere human act or answer, but in its clear ringing
simply is, and opens, on a purpose that has none,
for anybody who listens, everybody who listens –
is not an as-yet-undiscovered but recognisable corner
of Eden replanted into whatever moment *this* is,
unfallen from eternity yet focused full on this world
and made safe and familiar for human habitation?

And what then is dancing but the soul's call
to the body, with eyes as persuasive and invincible
as a recognised lover's, glistening with desire,
in one clear imperative: 'I want you. Take me. Now.'
And as feet in dancing can command the whole
being after them to abandon the planned evening,
the shop errand, the forced march, the predetermined journey
to the place of work, time of play, theatre of destruction,
whether via Central Station or the last tramway stop
at the outermost periphery of human possibility
and transform petty purpose into total celebration
of now in the cup of always, always in the bowl of now,

So also may this thin vessel pressed and spun
from non-human harmonies upon the wheel of language
and fired with images in a poem's kiln
resonate here on a single note called hope,
and overspill those sounds into this present
pouring music of impossibilities, rhythm of hallelujahs.
And may this blue creature stilled but alive on this page
move you again in the human dance named longing
and, by retouching also your hand from time to time,
allow these souls to dance and sing yet again.
Teach me, blue butterfly, to open
these winged words in singing and in dancing.

Things fall into place retrospectively

Seventh flight

Things fall into place retrospectively, and order is known where
                                           none seemed.
All I want is the impossible: to understand, even if not always.
Where a man treads lightly and fast, grazing time like wind on water,
and when fear of fear falls away, perhaps even the unknowable
may now and then be glimpsed. In interstices between passions,
in angles that form like spiders' webs below the ceilings of judgements,
between lines of action, in the ephemeral patterns criss-crossing
deserts of routine, in the wide skiey spaces of dreaming,
horizonless and surprising, and in each vernacular moment,
I affirm still a man may trace his particular vision
however vicarious or wavering, like the path
of a blue butterfly, write it fluent on tracks of air
and, however afraid at the outset, even of fear, to set out,
over lands, seas, skies of his individual passing,
register that, for always, in memory's palpable zone
for anybody who comes there, everybody who comes there,
to visit, to be touched by beauty, as one enters a garden.

Things fall into place retrospectively, and time is no
argument. The glimpse, the graze, the grasp,
the only true synchronicities, of the inner and outer combining.
To know them, to know one knows, and then to let go
of knowing, like this blue butterfly's flight
here in Šumarice, over these hills, this Maytime:
dance of the imago, I affirm, now, still and always.

7   Seven blessings

The burning butterfly

First blessing

Flames before me formed
a burning butterfly, who landed
on my lips.

I swallowed. His furry body
slid down my throat,
unresisting.

Leaf veined scaly dragon wings
scattering dust and perfume
dissolved on my tongue.

The corners of the mouth

Second blessing

I called: No, not this brine
leaking through cracked vessels
of pitted clay,

nor these hollow woodwind calls
from outworn flutes, seeping
in mortal echoes,

nor flesh and blood memorial
weaned or wound imperfect
from human hands,

but a cup of rock or bone
unmarrowed, non-porous, durable
against gales,

a black ring to bind speech, carved
in jet or onyx, to contain
the unsayable,

and a voice pure as impossible
harmony of human
made angel.

What seemed impossible

Third blessing

What seemed impossible
isn't. The black light behind the sun
opens. And on the skies, black stars.

Signet ring

Fourth blessing

Chiselled with metal pins, in miniature,
two butterflies hover. One, with whip and rein,
drives a two wheeled chariot, drawn by a pair
of long-tailed rodents. So is the human brain
drawn on by hope and longing, and controlled
by hovering psyche, we being rats, ensouled?

With merciless attention, being passionless,
the sure touch of one aerial charioteer
rests with no trace of pressure, haste or stress
on strings that guide direction, hope and fear.
The other, a pure pharaoh of the air,
surveying destiny, dances, and does not care.

True to your absence, glory

Fifth blessing

Is glory in the residue, mere evidence,
in shining track, in afterglow, in spoor?
Being too poor to meet you in your residence
I plead with glory, greet me at your door,
fully resplendent, present, now, revealed
hostlike to your *main tenant* in this space?
But you come always partially concealed
in mist, with indistinctly profiled face
hanging in haze, ghostlike. We shall remain
true to your absence, glory, seeing you are
bright only as a long exploded star,
a mote in darkness, spreading like a stain,
present but in the shrinking and the swelling,
their course in timespace, and their aftertelling.

Shalom

Sixth blessing

The unborn and the dead
gather in the head.

The dead and the unborn
fill plenty's horn

giving and forgiving
life for the living.

Grace

Seventh blessing

Under the hills, quiet
fire. From their graves
the dead awaken.

Blessing on you
who live, they call
through our own voices,

as in their places
we too shall call
our own unborn.

Under hills, this
grace flows
through everything.

Chestnut and oak
bud, green
earth's carpet.

Red tulip petals
scatter. A blue
butterfly hovers.

BELGRADE, ZEMUN, CAMBRIDGE
MAY 25, 1985–APRIL 27, 2006

Photographs and last messages

Mass arrest, Kragujevac, October 20, 1941

Confiscation of documents and belongings, outside the cannon sheds,
Šumarice, October 20, 1941, around 10 a.m.

*Prisoners being assembled before being led away to be shot, outside the cannon
sheds, Šumarice, October 21, 1941, probably between 7 a.m. and 2 p.m.*

Massacre, Šumarice, October 21, 1941

Last Messages

Dad – me and Miša are in the artillery barracks.
Bring us lunch, my jumper too and a rug.
Bring jam in a small jar
Paya
Dad see the Headmaster if it's worth it

Pavle Ivanović, aged 20,
grammar school student

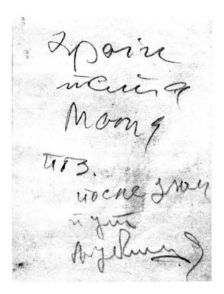

Dear mum and dad
hi for the last time.
Ljubiša

Ljubiša Jovanović, aged 17
grammar school pupil,
note scribbled into his school report book

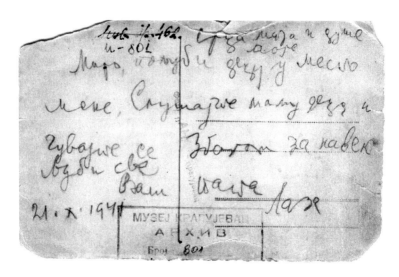

My sweetheart and my darlings
Mira kiss the children for me
Children listen to mum
and take care of yourselves
Goodbye for ever
Love your Dad Laza
21 Oct 1941

Lazar Pantelić, aged 48,
grammar school headmaster

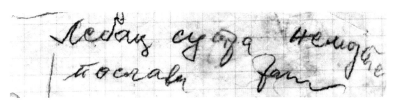

Don't send bread tomorrow

Jakov Medina, aged 56,
bookkeeper

Massacre, Šumarice, October 21, 1941

The Hanging of Stjepan Filipović, Valjevo, June 22, 1942

Postscript

Together with the notes that follow it, this postscript amplifies some aspects of *The Blue Butterfly*, in terms of biographical context, geographical setting and historical background.

INCEPTION

In May 1985, I visited Yugoslavia to run a series of poetry workshops for schoolchildren in towns and villages in central Serbia. My daughter Lara, then aged seventeen, accompanied me. We travelled by minibus with Serbian friends and colleagues to various locations. After a workshop at a school in Kragujevac on May 25, we were taken to the memorial museum of Šumarice, on the outskirts of the city, which commemorates the massacre by German occupiers on 19, 20 and 21 October, 1941.

It was *Dan mladosti* ['Youth Day'] in Titoist Yugoslavia, and the place was thronging with children on school outings. While we were queuing to enter the museum, a blue butterfly suddenly came to rest on the forefinger of my left hand – that is, my writing hand. Lara and I each had just enough time to take a photograph of the creature.

Immediately after our return to England, two poems wrote themselves out of me more or less spontaneously and in quick succession. These were the title poem (p. 8), followed almost immediately by 'Nada : Hope or Nothing' (p. 9). Sensing there was more to come, I embarked on a study of the history of the Second World War in Yugoslavia. The sequence began to unravel.

Two years later, a chance to work in Yugoslavia came up, and I jumped at it. When friends asked why I had decided on this move, my answer – *chasing butterflies* – wasn't entirely flippant. I wanted to find out as much as I could about the country.

My specific poetic intention was to write a long work, a book-length poem, which, even then, I sensed was being called, called for, from me, through me, out of me.

I lived in former Yugoslavia for three years, from July 1987 to June 1990. During that time, the structure of this book was mapped and some parts of it were completed.

Frontispiece

The detail shows the blue butterfly perched on the forefinger of my writing hand. The original snapshot was in colour. I took it with my clumsier right hand, while the butterfly was sunning itself on my left. The impression of lettering, that can just be made out in the background, is part of an inscription on the wall behind the glass door of the 21st October Memorial Museum. Although the exact words can't be seen from this print, they include Hitler's injunction to his occupying forces: *Machen Sie mir dieses Land deutsch*: 'Make this land German for me.'

The Species of Butterfly

The lack of definition in the photograph makes identification of the butterfly uncertain. After consulting descriptions and photographs in textbooks, I began to wonder if my butterfly might not be a *Maculinea arion* (Large Blue), which was then extinct in Britain.[1] When I sent emails to British butterfly experts, their replies explained that no positive identification was possible; that my butterfly was unlikely to be the Large Blue; and that it was in any case unlikely to be a native of the British Isles. But the Serbian entomologist Isidor Šarić was more forthcoming. He agreed that my amateur snapshot wasn't detailed enough for a conclusive identification. But he did suggest several possibilities: *Plebejus argyrognomon* (Reverdin's Blue); the rare *Polyommatus escheri* (Escher's Blue); *Agrodiaetus thersites* (Chapman's Blue); or one of the many variants of *Polyommatus icarus* (Common Blue). He pointed out that all these species are

[1] Since then, by transferring creatures from locations in Sweden, naturalists have successfully reintroduced the species to several sites in southern England.

to be found in the area of Kragujevac, and added that, out of 360 butterfly species in Europe, 200 of them are alive and well in Serbia. The cover of this book depicts a Common Blue.

KRAGUJEVAC, ŠUMADIJIA, ŠUMARICE

Šumadija [*šuma*, 'forest'] is a region of central and western Serbia. Its biggest city, Kragujevac [etym. *kraguj*, 'sparrowhawk'] lies at a natural crossroads on the river Lepenica, a tributary of the Morava. At the time of the 1941 massacre, swollen with refugees, its population was between 40,000 and 50,000.[2] In 1981, it was over 87,000; in 1991, over 147,000; and in 2005, over 211,000.

Šumarice ['Spinneys', from *šuma*, 'forest'] is an area outside Kragujevac, where the Nazi massacre took place on October 20 and 21, 1941. In pre-war years it had been a favourite place for picnics and outings. Part of it had been a First World War cemetery. In 1953, the whole site, including the cemetery, was cleared and converted into a Memorial Park. The 21st October Memorial Museum was opened there on February 15, 1976.

THE MASSACRE AT KRAGUJEVAC

During the Second World War, the German occupiers carried out group killings in many Serbian cities and towns, including Belgrade, Kraljevo, Pančevo, Šabac, Topola and Valjevo, as well as numerous villages. But the massacre at and around Kragujevac on October 19, 20 and 21, 1941 was the worst single atrocity of them all. It occurred six months after the Nazi invasion of Yugoslavia.

While the broad picture of what happened has been well established ever since the Nuremberg Trials of 1945–8, many aspects still remain controversial and a number of issues may never be completely clarified. At the risk of oversimplification, this account attempts to

[2] Figures provided by Slobodan Pavićević, email February 5, 2006. A contemporary German estimate of the population was 42,000. See the report written from Kragujevac by Reichskommandant Otto von Bischofshausen on October 20, 1941: http://forum.axishistory.com/viewtopic.php?p=5499 64&sid=7a114d22a9e2bcf264d89c28e85885b4. Accessed April, 2006.

collate some minimally accurate facts and interpretations. However, even this apparently straightforward intention is hard to accomplish. Misinformation, lying, spying, cheating and double-crossing were tactics deployed by all sides in the multiple struggles that swept Yugoslavia in the Second World War. The 'facts' turn out to be rigorously knotted in ideologies and, in some cases, to be so inextricable from them as to be deeply resistant to enquiry. As the leading authority on the Kragujevac massacre writes:

> Not one single objective study wholly devoted to the massacre in Kragujevac has been made to this day: that is, there has been no study properly based on documentation which would respect the requirements of historical science. However, some present or perhaps future researcher, freed from oppression, ideological prejudices and myth, is eventually bound to carry out this task for the sake of historical truth.[3]

OCCUPATION AND RESISTANCE

The Nazi invasion of Yugoslavia began on April 6, 1941, with a ferocious air attack on Belgrade that killed more than 5,000 civilians. The invasion was over in less than a fortnight. Isolated and more or less spontaneous incidents of rebellion started taking place in various parts of Yugoslavia as early as April 1941. By July and August, ambushes and acts of sabotage had increased and were being organised systematically. On August 4, 1941, General Heinrich Danckelmann, the military commander in Serbia, requested reinforcements to deal with the insurgency.

The specific events that precipitated the October massacre at Kragujevac resulted from an uneasy co-operation between the separate wings of resistance in Serbia: the nationalist and royalist *Četnici* ('Chetniks') of Colonel Dragoljub (Draža) Mihajlović, and

---

[3] Brkić, Staniša: 'The Tragedy of Kragujevac', unpublished monograph, 2006; kindly provided by the author, who began researching the massacre in 1982 and became Head of the 21st October Memorial Museum at Šumarice in 1992. Extract tr. Vera V. Radojević & RB. *Note added for 2nd edition*: The monograph was published in 2007 by Spomen-Park Kragujevački oktobar ['The Kragujevac October Memorial Park'], Kragujevac, entitled *Ime i broj*: *Kragujevacka tragedija 1941* ['*Number and name: the Kragujevac Tragedy 1941*'].

the Yugoslav Communist Party under the command of Josip Broz (Tito).[4]

Felix Benzler, the German Plenipotentiary (Foreign Minister) in Belgrade, was well aware of the potential for Communist-Chetnik co-operation. In a telegram to the German Foreign Ministry in Berlin, dated August 12 and marked 'Top Secret', he wrote:

> Collaboration between the Chetnik leadership and the Communists has not yet been encountered, but the Communists are seeking to influence the Chetnik rank and file with false slogans and in some instances by coercive means, successfully as the Military Commander has learned. In case the Chetniks make common cause with the Communists, it will not be possible to use the Serbian gendarmerie.[5]

A month later, Hitler himself decided to deal swiftly and decisively with an insurgency that was threatening to turn into a mass uprising. In a 'Führer's Directive' dated September 16, 1941, he issued instructions for 'the task of crushing the insurrectionary movement' and ordered General Franz Böhme to be transferred from Greece to carry it out.[6] A former Austrian military officer, a Catholic, and a veteran of World War I, Böhme arrived in Serbia on September 19, 1941. He issued strict numerical criteria for the selection of male victims for execution in reprisal against attacks on German officers, soldiers and members of the German ethnic minority ('Volksdeutschers'): 100 for each German killed and 50 for each German wounded.[7]

---

[4] See the entry for *Četnik, Četnici* in the glossary: p. 149.
[5] *Documents on German Foreign Policy, 1918–1945, Series D, Vol. XIII, The War Years, June 23, 1941–December 11, 1941*, Her Majesty's Stationery Office, London, 1964, p. 308.
[6] *Documents on German Foreign Policy, 1918–1945, Series D, Vol. XIII, The War Years, June 23, 1941–December 11, 1941*, Her Majesty's Stationery Office, London, 1964, p. 517. Böhme relieved Danckelmann as Military Commander in Serbia and held the post until December 2, 1941.
[7] See 'Standing Orders', p. 4 above, and the note, p. 141–2 below.

The attack that provoked the massacre took place in the village of Ljuljaci, which lies on the highway between Kragujevac and Gornji Milanovac, between 2 and 3 a.m. on October 16, 1941.[9] There were 9 German soldiers killed and 27 wounded, of whom one died later.[10] Those involved in the attack on the German platoon were both Chetniks and Communists, operating in exactly the kind of "uneasy co-operation" mentioned above.[11]

In the following two days, mass arrests took place in Kragujevac. In accordance with Böhme's directives, Major Otto Desch, Commander of the 749th Regiment, issued the order to carry out reprisals. This was delivered to two other officers, each in charge of a battalion: Captain Fritz Fiedler of the 3rd Battalion of the 749th Regiment, and Major Paul König of the 1st Battalion of the 724th. The latter was charged with overall responsibility for the executions.

On the basis of a list which the City Police had received from Belgrade on Saturday, October 18, two groups were arrested in Kragujevac in the evening. The first consisted of 53 common prisoners, and the second of Jews, nationalists, communists and communist 'sympathisers'.[12]

---

[8] Much of the following documentary information relies on published and unpublished essays by Staniša Brkić, kindly provided by him for this postscript.

[9] Brkić, Staniša: The Tragedy of Kragujevac', unpublished monograph, 2006.

[10] von Bischofshausen, Otto: report, October 20, 1941.

[11] For a closely argued but highly polemical presentation on the relative roles and claims of the two groups in this battle, see Kostadinović, Slobodan: 'Le martyre de Kragujevac en octobre 1941': http://www.pogledi.co.yu/francuski/kg.php. Accessed, February–April, 2006.

[12] Two contemporary reports by German officers give different accounts of the numbers in the second group. Von Bischofshausen writes that 70 people were arrested (report, October 20). Major Paul König, Commander of the 1st Battalion of the 724th Regiment, mentions 66 Jews, communists and nationalists (report to the 724th Regiment, October 27). In a third post-War report, to the Yugoslav State Commission, the Mayor of Kragujevac, Dragomir Simović stated that 63 men and women had been arrested. Source: Brkić, Staniša, unpublished monograph, 2006.

THE MASSACRE

On Sunday, October 19, under the respective command of Fiedler and König, troops of the 1st and 3rd Battalions shot a total of 411 people in the nearby villages of Maršić, Mećkovac [*aka* Ilićevo), Grošnica and Beloševac.[13]

On the same day, the High Command of the 749th Regiment decided that further executions needed to be carried out in Kragujevac itself.[14] Members of Dimitrije Ljotić's collaborationist *Srpski dobrovoljački odred* ['Serbian Volunteer Detachment', also known as *Ljotićevci*) had arrived in Kragujevac on October 16 and 17, respectively from Belgrade and Arandjelovac, and they were actively involved in helping the Nazis.[15] They busied themselves by doing the dirty work of rounding up their fellow Serbs all over the town.[16]

---

[13] 'According to Major König, 427 men were shot. In this estimate of the victims, he must have included those who survived, on the grounds that all of them had been taken out to be shot. Von Bischofshausen, in his report dated October 20, states that 422 people were killed. In the 21st October Memorial Museum, details have been gathered to date of 411 men who were killed and of 21 survivors.' Brkić, Staniša: unpublished monograph, 2006. Tr. Vera V. Radojević & RB.

[14] Von Bischofshausen's report, which was written on October 20 (the day immediately after the reprisal killings in the villages), warned against further reprisals in Kragujevac itself: 'According to my point of view, the shooting of people from this city, some of whom are entirely innocent, may have directly harmful effects. It is to be expected that embittered relatives of those shot will now practise acts of revenge on members of the German armed forces.' For the source, see footnote 2 above. Tr. slightly changed by RB.

[15] See the glossary for entries on *Srpski dobrovoljački odred, Ljotićevci* and *ZBOR*, pp. 151–2. On the involvement of Ljotić's men in the marshalling of victims at Kragujevac, see also Kostadinović, Slobodan: 'Le martyre de Kragujevac en octobre 1941', http://www.pogledi.co.yu/francuski/kg.php. 'The whole of Kragujevac saw them as they went about assembling citizens so they could take part in the selection of those who were to be shot in reprisals.' Extract tr. from French, RB; accessed, February–April, 2006.

[16] After the massacre, The *ljotićevci* were also involved in guarding several hundred survivors, who had been spared by the Germans so that they could be used as forced labour to bury the dead. Source: Brkić, Staniša, unpublished monograph, 2006.

The mass killings over the next two days took place in Šumarice. Once again, König and Fiedler supervised the proceedings. The precise locations of the shootings, which were carefully chosen in order to minimise escape, were low-lying places where there were several small streams and ditches.[17] This account of what happened on October 20 and 21, 1941, is from a publication put out by the Memorial Park:

> All entries to and exits from the town were blocked. Arrests started on October 20. People were arrested in their homes, on the streets, and in shops and factories. Pupils and their teachers were taken out of their classes at school. There was almost no resistance to the arrests because the Germans claimed that it was all being done in order to renew personal identity documents. There were individual cases of people who had evaded the first wave of arrests but voluntarily gave themselves up to the Germans later. Several thousand people were arrested and imprisoned in the barracks of a former artillery regiment on the outskirts of the town. Most of them never even suspected that they were going to be shot. They thought the worst that could happen to them was that they would be sent to labour camps in Germany. However, with the dusk of October 20 came the first bursts of machine-gun fire. A group of 123 men and women were executed, consisting mostly of the hostages, nationalists, communists and Jews who had been arrested previously. Nine people managed to survive this shooting. One of them was Živojin Jovanović, who appeared at Nuremberg in 1947 to testify as a witness of the crimes in Kragujevac. At seven in the morning on October 21, the doors of the barracks were opened and groups were taken out to be shot. By two o'clock in the afternoon, the execution was complete. According to the data at our disposal, thirty-one men survived the execution. Some of the imprisoned were released, while the others were kept as hostages [. . .] While the machine-guns echoed through Šumarice, Kragujevac was silent, only to break out in the weeping and mourning of wailing mothers, wives, sisters and children. The groups of stragglers who were released to go home, entered the town with heads bowed, cursing their destiny and wishing they had been killed

---

[17] 'The place of execution, in the low lying area of the Sušički and Erdoglijski streams in Šumarice, was carefully selected. It is very hard to get away from these valleys, but to make sure that everything went according to plan, a machine gun was positioned at each of the main advantage points along the slopes overlooking these streams.' Brkić, Staniša, unpublished monograph, 2006. Tr. Vera V. Radojević and RB.

too. The next day, Kragujevac was blackened by the flags hanging from the houses and the scarves on women's heads.[18]

Within eight days of these events, Benzler in Belgrade concluded that aspects of the reprisals had been mismanaged. On October 29, he wrote another telegram marked 'Top Secret' to the German Foreign Ministry:

[. . .] In the past week there have been executions without trial of a large number of Serbs, not only in Kraljevo but also in Kragujevac, as reprisals for the killing of members of the Wehrmacht in the proportion of 100 Serbs for one German. In Kraljevo 1,700 male Serbs were executed, in Kragujevac 2,300. [. . .] Mistakes have been made in the executions. Thus confidential agents, Croats, and the entire personnel of German armament plants have been shot.[19] [. . .] The executions in Kragujevac occurred although there had been no attacks on members of the Wehrmacht in this city, for the reason that not enough hostages could be found elsewhere.

[18] Brkić, Staniša: *Kragujevačka tragedija / Kragujevac Tragedy*, bilingual booklet, Kragujevac October Memorial Park, undated. Tr. Tatjana Grujić, with emendations and corrections by RB.

[19] Kragujevac had been a centre for arms production since the foundation of a cannon foundry in 1851, which was expanded into a factory called the *Vojno tehnički zavod* ['Military Technical Bureau'] in 1853. The *Vojno tehnički zavod* marked the beginning of Kragujevac's industrial growth and set the entire tone and pattern for the city's development over the next 150 years as a centre for heavy industry: first armaments and munitions, then trucks and cars, then chemicals and pharmaceuticals. (See Todorović, Dragan, Radovanović, Zoran & Kukić, Emilija: 'Military Production In Serbia', *Vreme News Digest Agency*, No 294, May 24, 1997: http://www. scc.rutgers.edu/serbian_digest/294/t294-3.htm. Accessed February 2006.) In 1941, it is likely that the Kragujevac industries were of considerable military and industrial importance to the Germans.

The factory was reconstituted after the Second World War under the name *Crvena Zastava* ['Red Flag'], and later simply as *Zastava*. Since the late 1950s, it has been best known for car production. The continuing involvement of the *Zastava* industrial complex in munitions was the motive attributed to NATO for the bombing of the city on March 24, 1999. See such references as http://www.emergency.com/1999/serbia04. htm ; and http://www.cnn.com/WORLD/europe/9904/09/nato. attack.04/: accessed, February, 2006. The location chosen for a mass protest rally on March 31, 1999, was the site of the Šumarice massacre.

These indiscriminate executions are causing repercussions among the population which are contrary to our final political objective. They have also made Prime Minister Nedić uncertain in setting his objectives.

The Plenipotentiary Commanding General has thereupon issued new directives concerning the execution of hostages, which do not change anything in the ratio of one hundred Serbs for one German, to be sure, but eliminate as far as possible mistakes such as those mentioned above.[20]

THE VICTIMS: FICTION AND MYTH

Since the Nuremberg Trials, there have been many different accounts of the numbers of victims at Kragujevac. Among these, the figure of 7,000 has resonated through semi-official and popular narratives both in Serbia and internationally. This well-rounded, easily memorable number has taken on the status of a symbol, even of a myth.[21] Today, it is still to be found quoted repeatedly, for example, in the *Encyclopaedia Britannica* entry on Kragujevac, as in many other such reference sources.

The first time this number is known to have been documented is in a sentence written in the margin of the *minej* ['*Menaion*'] by Dragoslav Veličković, vicar of the Kragujevac *Stara crkva* ['Old Church']: 'On today's date, 1941, the Germans executed about 7,000 citizens of Kragujevac by gunfire.'[22] Allegedly, this figure was repeated at Nuremberg in the eyewitness account of the survivor Živojin Jovanović, although on one occasion he is known to have changed his testimony to a count of 8,000 victims.[23]

The large discrepancies between the latest and most objective Serbian accounts of the total number of murdered victims, the orig-

[20] *Documents on German Foreign Policy, 1918–1945, Series D, Vol. XIII, The War Years, June 23, 1941–December 11, 1941*, Her Majesty's Stationery Office, London, 1964, pp. 708–9.

[21] This was the version of the story I was told on my first visit to Kragujevac in 1985. See the note on 'The blue butterfly', p. 143 below.

[22] The 'Menaion' is the monthly book of offices and services in the Slavonic Orthodox Churches. Source: Brkić, Staniša, unpublished monograph, 2006.

[23] Brkić, Staniša: unpublished monograph, 2006. Source: Reg. no. 9, copy of translation of the Nuremberg Trial, *Arhiv Vojno-Istorijskog Instituta (AVII)* ['Military History Museum Archive'], Belgrade.

inal German estimates, and the popularly accepted estimate of 7,000, do call for some explanation. At least five possible factors may be suggested. First, that the Germans deliberately destroyed evidence. Second, that the numbers *appeared* huge to surviving witnesses.[24] Third, that through hearsay and word-of-mouth reports, the ubiquitous sense of wrong and persecution released after the war among the survivors of the occupation, both in Šumadija and throughout Yugoslavia, magnified perception of the numbers of those killed. Fourth, similarly, that in the popular mind, the many victims in smaller town and villages in the area around and near Kragujevac were conflated with the numbers who died at Šumarice itself. And fifth, that the post-war Communist government kept quiet about the figures established by the experts, and built on the tragedy for propaganda purposes, magnifying the atrocity in order to unite the population behind its policies.[25]

---

[24] Glišić, Venceslav: 'When determining an approximate number for the victims of Kragujevac, one should bear two points in mind. First, the Germans did all they could to hide the truth from world opinion about this grievous crime of theirs. For this reason, by the end of 1943, they had destroyed all lists of executed persons. Second, those individuals who survived to give testimony were so overwhelmingly impressed by the huge crowds of people who had been rounded up, as well as by the entire tragic nature of the procedure, that, under the influence of these impressions, they estimated that there were more than 7,000 victims.' Source: Brkić, Staniša, unpublished monograph, 2006. Extract tr. Vera V. Radojević & RB.

[25] See, for example, Kostadinović, Slobodan: 'Le martyre de Kragujevac en octobre 1941': http://www.pogledi.co.yu/francuski/kg.php. Kostadinović advocates the strong version of a conspiracy theory: that in purges following the liberation of October 1944, when old scores were settled against both collaborators and royalists, Tito's post-war government deliberately masked its own secret murders of its opponents by exaggerating the numbers of citizens who had been killed by the Germans three years earlier. Accessed, February–April, 2006.

Finally, there may also have been a further, much simpler economic motive: swelling the numbers of war victims in order to maximise Yugoslav claims against Germany for war reparations.

THE VICTIMS: FACTS

Over the years, and especially since the collapse of the Yugoslav Federation in the late 1980s, researchers at the 21st October Memorial Museum have made detailed and painstaking enquiries. They have accumulated a large body of evidence, all of which has now been computerised, a process that enables stricter cross-checking and considerably greater accuracy. The result of this research is a carefully worded statement:

> In our unofficial sources, estimates of the number of people killed range from 3,000 to 8,000. The State Commission for war crimes in Kragujevac, which was set up in 1945, verified that 2,324 people were shot on 20 and 21 October 1941. This figure does not include the victims who were killed in the surrounding villages [. . .] Basing its figures on research into all available sources, the 21st October Memorial Museum has at its disposal the data that 2,797 men, women and children were executed: 411 victims on 19 October, 114 on 20 October and 2,272 on 21 October. According to the research so far completed, 61 people survived the executions.[26]

Several further details and qualifications were provided by Staniša Brkić in answer to specific enquiries of mine:

> [. . .] 27 women were shot or lost their lives in some other way in Kragujevac on 19, 20 and 21 October. The number of female victims has not been completely researched.[27]

> [. . .] In the group of 70, there were 40 Jews.[28]

> [. . .] 25 children aged between 12 and 15 were shot in Kragujevac on 21 October and one boy in a village on 19 October: a total of 26 children. But [. . .] this is only conditionally correct.

---

[26] Brkić, Staniša: *Kragujevačka tragedija / Kragujevac Tragedy*, bilingual booklet, The Kragujevac October Memorial Park, undated. Extract retranslated by Vera V. Radojević & RB.

[27] Pavičević, Slobodan: email, January 26, 2006; based on information provided by Staniša Brkić. Tr. Vera V. Radojević & RB.

[28] This refers to the first group arrested in Kragujevac on October 18, who were killed on October 19. See note 12, p. 128 above.

[. . .] Not all of them were boys, there were also five girls.[29]

[. . .] 217 children of secondary school age were shot, including pupils from all the schools in the town, as well as others in the same age group who were no longer at school: farm workers, labourers, apprentices, etc. This number also includes several individuals who were older than 19 but for whom documentation exists to show that they were still attending school.

[. . .] the oldest person killed was Novak Lučić, aged 78, and the youngest executed was Dragiša Nikolić, born December 20, 1929 (aged 11).

[. . .] It is quite certain that the evidence on the number of persons killed cannot be definitive and that, as far as this issue is concerned, no final conclusion is ever likely to be reached. Even now, during the course of research, details are still emerging about individuals who were killed, even though they were never previously listed. Certain names have also had to be removed from the list, in cases when it has been documented and proved that they were not killed.[30]

Desanka Maksimović

In Serbia, the best known poem about the massacre at Kragujevac is 'Krvava bajka' ['Bloody Fable' or 'Bloody Fairy Tale'] by Desanka Maksimović (1898–1993).[31] According to a book of interviews with her, the poem was written on the day after the massacre, when an old man stopped her in the street near her house in Belgrade and 'agitatedly, without any introduction or greeting', accosted her and said: 'Do you know what has happened in Kragujevac?'

> Not mentioning the mass shooting of the grown-ups, the old man told me how the Germans had burst into the grammar school and taken several classes of pupils straight out of their lessons to be shot. Then he rushed off without saying goodbye to me, as if he was going from one room to another and would be back in a second [. . .] That man, whom I met by chance, was the bearer of the most heartrend-

[29] Brkić, Staniša: email, March 3, 2006, tr. Vera V. Radojević.
[30] Brkić, Staniša: unpublished monograph, 2006.
[31] The poem was first published in the magazine *Naša književnost* ['Our Literature'], Belgrade, 1946.

ing and terrible news for me. I had the feeling that he would go on broadcasting the news along all the streets of Belgrade until the end of that day, unless the Germans killed him somewhere along the way. And that is why I think of him as the co-author of 'Krvava bajka', the poem I wrote in a single breath. The poem was born quickly and easily, just as when a tear falls, just as if one were sighing [. . .] As I wrote 'Krvava bajka', I was trembling with pain [. . .] I wrote it in a kind of awed terror, on that 23rd October. I was afraid that my pen might disturb any of it. Let it stay like that, I thought, as if I'd been crying, wailing [. . .] At that moment I had the need to feel that those children had not vanished, that they were still alive somewhere. I desperately wanted to protect myself: to believe that they were all still floating somewhere in the clouds. As in religion, though there was nothing religious about it.[32]

Lines from Desanka Maksimović's poem are inscribed on a roughly hewn slab of stone at the site of the massacre. Before the collapse of Yugoslavia, this poem was textbook reading for schoolchildren throughout the Federation.

'The Great Lesson'

Kragujevac was liberated on the third anniversary of the massacre, October 21, 1944. On the following day, the first requiem was held for the victims, in the presence of thousands of people.[33] In 1957, a cultural event entitled *Veliki školski čas* [the 'Big School Lesson' or 'Great Lesson'] was inaugurated in the city.[34] The name itself refers to the deaths of the hundreds of schoolchildren, and the seventeen teachers from local schools who went out to die along with their pupils. By 1959, the event had started to attract writers, actors, artists, singers and public figures from all the Yugoslav republics and, on October 21, 1962, for the first time under this name, a memorial ceremony was held in Šumarice. Since 1964, *Veliki školski čas* has

[32] Ljubisav Andrić, *Sa Desankom Maksimović* ['*With Desanka Maksimović*], Matica srpska, Novi Sad, 1984, pp. 115–120. Slobodan Pavičević drew my attention to this account: email, January 29, 2006. Extract tr. Vera V. Radojević & RB.
[33] Brkić, Staniša: unpublished monograph, 2006.
[34] These and some of the following details in this account were provided by Slobodan Pavičević: emails, January and February, 2006.

been commemorated on this anniversary every year, in front of the memorial to the schoolboys who were shot.

There are many stories of individual heroism. A poem entitled 'Kragujevac' by Radoje Radovanović, published in Belgrade in 1947, was influential in the development of this annual event, as was 'Krvava bajka' by Desanka Maksimović, who was herself a secondary school teacher of Serbian language and literature.[35] Radovanović's poem was dedicated to the memory of Miloje Pavlović, also a teacher of Serbian, and Principal of the *Ženska učiteljska škola* ['Women's Teacher Training School']. Pavlović was 54 years old when he was killed. The final line of Radovanović's poem renders Pavlović's last words as '*Pucajte. Ja i sada držim čas*'.[36] The line is inscribed on a stone slab at the Šumarice site. Although no witnesses survived to report what Pavlović actually said to his pupils as he led them out to be shot, in the post-war years in Yugoslavia this line gradually became an ineradicable part of national folklore. It caught the mood of the times in a dignified and appropriate way, and distilled whatever cathartic and positive meaning could be drawn for the townspeople, especially the families of the murdered men and boys, not to mention for the population as a whole.

Another teacher who died heroically at Šumarice was Lazar Pantelić, vice-principal of the *Prva muška gimnazija* ['First Boys' Grammar School']. He taught biology. Born in the town of Šabac on February 5, 1893, he was 48 years old when he was killed. He left a widow and five children aged between 11 and 16. For reasons that are unclear, on the day of the massacre Pantelić was put into the group designated not be executed. But when he saw that some of his pupils were among those who were going to be shot, he asked if he could take their place. When he was refused, he insisted on joining them. So he walked out to his death voluntarily in front of the boys in his class.[37]

---

[35] See p. 135–6 above.
[36] In the poem 'Don't Send Bread Today', the Serbian line has been rendered as: '*Go ahead. Shoot. I am giving my lesson. Now.*' See p. 6.
[37] For his last scribbled message to his wife and children, see p. 118 above. In 'Don't send bread tomorrow' (p. 6), the stories of the deaths of Pavlović and Pantelić and the line from Radovanović have been conflated.

Between 1971 and 1990, *Veliki školski čas* usually consisted of the performance of an oratorio commissioned from a Yugoslav composer, with words by a Yugoslav poet, before an open-air audience of around 60,000 people. Each year, a poet from a different republic of the Federation was chosen. On October 21, 1988, in an attempt to emphasise the event's international significance, work by three non-Yugoslav poets was included in the performance, to represent both Eastern and Western blocs and the countries in the 'Non-Aligned' movement. The poets were Pjotr Vegin (USSR), Amrita Pritam (India) and myself (UK). Extracts were taken from the title-poem, 'The Blue Butterfly', translated by Danilo Kiš and Ivan V. Lalić.

Since 1990, following the break-up of Yugoslavia, *Veliki školski čas* has been a more modest affair, not an international event.

RB
CAMBRIDGE
APRIL 27, 2006

Added for the second edition

THE NUMBER SEVEN

As the above text clarifies, the figure of 7,000 victims popularised in many accounts of the Kragujevac massacres does not correspond to the historical facts. It is a fact, however, that this figure rapidly became widely accepted and took on quasi-mythical status. Certainly, when I first visited Kragujevac in 1985, like most people I was told that 7,000 people had been killed. There seemed no reason not to accept this version.

In retrospect, I think that the figure of 7,000 itself affected me during the composition of *The Blue Butterfly*, above all when the sequence structured itself into seven parts, each containing seven poems – even though I can't say for sure at which point this numerological structure first appeared in my mind. I mention this now, not in an attempt to provide a plausible but reductive explanation for the patternings in the book, but because I think that the figure 7,000 did trigger composition in a particular direction. I think this is to do with the symbolic resonances and psychological associations of the number seven. These are immensely rich and deep. [38]

An additional direct effect on composition was that in early versions of several poems, especially those written in the 1980s and early 1990s, the number seven cropped up explicitly in several poems. And although I was in possession of the correct facts by the time it came to preparing the first edition of this book, and even though I believed I had corrected or changed all of these figures, several instances of this phrasing still somehow slipped past my attention during proofreading and persisted on surfacing into the text. Clearly these numbers had rooted themselves in me in their own right, whether as 'forms' or 'images' or both.

For the sake of factual truth, for this second edition I have changed the phrasing in all but one of these instances. In the 'Notes'

---

[38] See for example the copious exploration of the number seven in *Dictionary of Symbols*, Jean Chevalier and Alain Gheerbrant, tr. J. Buchanan-Brown, Penguin Books, 1996, pp. 859–866; and in *Elsevier's Dictionary of Symbols and Imagery*, Ad De Vries, revised and updated by Arthur de Vries, Amsterdam, 2004, pp. 505–506.

that follow this 'Postscript', for each of the poems affected, the earlier phrasings are now indicated: see the entries below, on 'The blue butterfly' (p. 143), 'The telling, third attempt' (p. 144), 'First wreath' (p. 144) and 'Third wreath (p. 144). However, from 'non-factual' perspectives, I am not so sure that these changes have always meant 'improvements'. And in one particular poem, 'Fifth wreath' (p. 144), the word 'seven' is crucial to both meaning and patterning. There, I have kept the original phrasing. As far as this anomaly is concerned, then, the text of *The Blue Butterfly* is flawed by a (slight, but inevitable?) instability.

'THE GREAT LESSON' 2007

On 21st October 2007, *The Blue Butterfly* was selected as the theme-text for the annual commemorative event at the site of the massacre in Šumarice Memorial Park. The entire *Veliki školski čas* event was broadcast on national television, as poems from the Serbian translation were recited and sung before a large open-air audience.[39]

RB
CAMBRIDGE
JULY 7, 2008

---

[39] *Plavi leptir* (*The Blue Butterfly*), tr. Vera. V. Radojević, with two poems translated by Danilo Kiš and Ivan V. Lalić, and accompanied by two essays by Slobodan Rakitić and Srba Ignjatović; published by Kragujevački oktobar ['Kragujevac October'], Kraguejvac, in association with Plava tačka ['Blue Spot'], Belgrade, 2007.

Notes

DEDICATION
For the Living. This is the translation of the title of a booklet about the massacre, *Živima* (Kragujevac, 1976). *The Blue Butterfly* is also dedicated to the memory of all those killed in the massacre and to the members of their families who survived them.

EPIGRAPH: ZHUANG ZHOU (CHUANG-TSU)
Variously translated. This version is mine.

STAGNATION, p. 3
Based on Hexagram 12 of *Yijing* (*I Ching*). Composed in Cambridge around 1985–6.

TWO DOCUMENTS, pp. 4–5
These 'found poems' were transcribed in Cambridge in the early 1990s. The 'Standing Orders' were issued by Franz Böhme, German commanding General in Serbia from September 19 to December 2, 1941. The 'Report' was submitted by Böhme to General Walter Kuntze, who on October 24, 1941, was temporarily assigned to the post of Deputy Commander, Southeast, and Commander-in-Chief of the 12th German Army, to replace General Wilhelm List. Others directly above Böhme in the chain of Nazi command included Kuntze, List, Chief of the German General Staff Wilhelm Keitl and, ultimately, Hitler himself. The 'Standing Orders' are quoted from *The Kragujevac October Memorial Park*, Kragujevac, 1985. The 'Report' is quoted from Hehn, Paul E.: *The German Struggle Against Yugoslav Guerrillas in World War II, German Counter-Insurgency in Yugoslavia 1941–1943*, Columbia University Press, New York, 1979.

Keitel was tried at Nuremberg and executed on 16th October 1946. Böhme was captured on May 9, 1945 in Norway. Along with List and Kuntze, he was to be put on trial at Nuremberg in the so-called 'Hostages Trial' or 'Southeast Case' (Case No. 7), for war crimes and crimes against humanity committed in Serbia, specifically in Kragujevac and its adjoining towns and villages. Indictments were filed on May 10, 1947. But on May 29, prior to his arraignment, he committed suicide by jumping off the fourth floor of his prison. The trial lasted from July 15, 1947 until February 19, 1948. Sentences were confirmed on January 18, 1949. List was sentenced to life imprisonment, released on parole in 1951 because of ill health, and died twenty years later in Garmisch, Bavaria. Kuntze received the same sentence, and was also released on medical parole, on February 10, 1953. He died in 1968. See: http://www.trumanlibrary.org/whistlestop/study_collec tions/nuremberg/documents/index.php?documentdate=1947-07-15&documentid=C192-9-1&studycollectionid=&pagenumber=1. Accessed March 2006.

<small>DON'T SEND BREAD TOMORROW</small>, pp. 6–7
Italicised lines are taken from messages scribbled by victims, on any available scraps of paper they could find, as they awaited execution. 41 messages were discovered. Several were written on postcards and one inside a school report book. Some messages were dated, some not. Most were written in the old artillery barracks at Stanovljansko polje ['Stanovljansko Field'], on the outskirts of Kragujevac, where prisoners were locked up before being marched off to be massacred several hundred metres away at Šumarice. Some messages were found scattered on the ground. Some were found in victims' pockets before burial.

The fragments of messages are translated as literally as possible, though the Serbian is usually more economical and therefore poignant than it is possible to render here. Nor is English as rich in intimacies as Serbian. The full message from the headmaster, Lazar Pantelić, to his wife and children, which is translated as 'My sweetheart and my darlings', actually starts with the tenderer endearments: *Srca moja i duše moje*, literally 'My heart and my souls' (see p. 118).

The victims whose words appear in the poem are: Pavle Ivanović, aged 20, grammar school student (lines 7–10); Bogoljub Gligorijević, aged 39, merchant, (lines 11–12); Novica Milanović, foundry worker, aged 30 (lines 19–20); Dragoljub Vasović, aged 42, cobbler (line 21); Borivoje Pavlović, aged 33, welder (lines 22–23); Stevan Vuleta, aged 45, worker (line 24); Dobrivoje Milošević, aged 37, worker (line 31); Lazar Pantelić, aged 48, headmaster (line 32); Svetislav Miljković, aged 39, coffee-shop owner (lines 33–34); Sava Stefanović, aged 44, master gunsmith; (line 35); and Jakov Medina, aged 56, bookkeeper (line 36 and the title). The message from Jakov Medina, incidentally, is addressed in the second person plural (*Nemojte* – 'Don't'), which indicates either formality or more than one recipient. Line 18 is attributed to Miloje Pavlović, aged 54, college principal: see p. 137 above.

The student Pavle Ivanović was arrested on 18 October, imprisoned in the barracks and shot in a group together with the town's Jews, on 20 October. The same probably applies to Bogoljub Gligorijević. Most of the others are thought to have been killed on 21 October.

This poem is dedicated to Stanisa Brkić, who generously provided the photographs and documents reproduced on pp. 113–120, and much of the information in the Postscript and in these notes. Some of these messages were published in the booklet, *For The Living* (21st October Memorial Museum, Kragujevac, 1976) and in Brkić, Staniša & Djordjević, Nenead: *Veliki zločni Vermahta* ['The Great Crimes of the Wehrmacht'], *Kragujevac 1941* (21st October Memorial Museum, Kragujevac, undated). See also THE GREAT LESSON', pp. 136–137 above. Drafts for this poem were made in Cambridge and Belgrade, in 1985 and 1990. It was completed on April 18, 2006.

THE BLUE BUTTERFLY, p. 8
Written in Cambridge, May–June 1985. The seventh stanza in this poem was altered on February 20, 2006 for the first edition of this book. After spending much of January 2006 re-reading my original source material and exploring more recent historical evidence, I realised that the lines in stanza 7 about the numbers of victims had to be changed if I was to give an honest and accurate account. See THE VICTIMS, pp. 132–135 and THE NUMBER SEVEN, p. 139. In the early publications of the poem, this stanza read:
> On my proud firm hand, miraculously
> Blessed by the seven thousand martyred
> Men and boys fallen at Kragujevac,

This poem was translated into Serbian by Ivan. V. Lalić and Danilo Kiš (*Veliki školski čas*, No. 19, Kragujevac, 1987; and *Braničevo*, Požarevac, May 1988) and, separately, also by Moma Dimić and Ivan Gadjanski. A documentary programme about the poem was made for Yugoslav national television by the poet and broadcaster Duška Vrhovac (Belgrade, 1989).

NADA : HOPE OR NOTHING, p. 9
Nada : 'hope' in Serbo-Croatian; 'nothing' in Spanish. The last line of the poem lists the word 'hope' in Serbo-Croat, Greek, Russian, Spanish and German. Written in Cambridge, May–June 1985. Translated into Serbo-Croat by Ivan V. Lalić (*Oktobar*, No 22, Kraljevo, 1988) and into Macedonian by M. Čenaroski (*Razgledi*, Skopje, May 1989).

THE TELLING, pp. 10–15
Dedicated to Slobodan Pavičević. Drafted and polished between 1987 and 2001, in Belgrade, Zemun and Cambridge. 'The telling, third

attempt' was translated into Serbo-Croat by Daša Marić (*Oktobar*, No. 22, Kraljevo, 1988; *Odzivi*, Bijelo Polje, December 1989) and Macedonian by M. Čenaroski (*Razgledi*, Skopje, May 1989).

Until the second edition of this book, in all versions of 'The telling, third attempt', p. 14, the fifth line of the second stanza read: 'souls of seven thousand dead men at rest'. For discussion on the numbers of the dead, see THE VICTIMS, pp. 132–135 and THE NUMBER SEVEN, p. 139 above.

WAR AGAIN : YUGOSLAVIA 1991, p. 16
Written, Cambridge, 1991.

THE DEATH OF CHILDREN, pp. 19–25
Prompted by the accidental deaths of three young people in Split, January 4, 1988. They were standing at a bus stop when a wall fell and crushed them. It turned out that the concrete in the structure hadn't been properly reinforced. The poems are dedicated to their memories: Andrea Filipić, Ljubica Glavica and Marin Miloš, and for their families and friends. Composed, Belgrade, January 6–11, 1988.

SEVEN WREATHS, pp. 29–35
Drafted and polished between 1987 and 2005, in Belgrade, Zemun and Cambridge, and revisited in 2008.

In the first edition of this book, three poems mentioned the number seven. In two of these instances, I have changed the earlier phrasing for subsequent editions. In FIRST WREATH (p. 29, line 1), 'From what remains of seven thousand dead' now becomes 'From what remains of the Kragujevac dead'; and in THIRD WREATH (p. 31, line 4), 'seven thousand' has been changed to 'three thousand'. But in FIFTH WREATH (p. 33, line 2), I finally decided not to change the word 'seven' because pattern and meaning depend on this word, even though the result is inconsistent. For further discussion on the numbers of the dead, see THE VICTIMS, pp. 132–135 and THE NUMBER SEVEN, pp. 139–140 above.

THE SHADOW WELL, p. 39
Composed in Cambridge, September 5–6, 1995, based on earlier notes; completed, December 24, 1997 & January 29, 1998. Translated into Serbian by Srba Mitrović (*Kletva*, Serbian Writers' Association, 1999).

WHEN NIGHT COVERED EUROPE, pp. 40–41
Composed, 1987–8, in Belgrade.

BALLAD OF THE SEAGULL : THE SCHOOLBOY pp. 42–44
Written in Belgrade, Zemun and Cambridge, between 1989 and 1997.

From 'Mauthausen', pp. 45–46
Translated from the Greek poet and dramatist Iakovos Kampanellis (1922–2011). In 1940, Kampanellis was involved in anti-Nazi resistance and tried to escape, first to the Middle East and then to Switzerland, through Austria, where he was arrested and deported to the Mauthausen concentration camp. He was imprisoned in the camp until May 5, 1945, when it was liberated by the Allies. The poems were set to music by Mikis Theodorakis for his song-cycle *Mauthausen*, performed by Maria Farandouri, in 1965. These versions were made in Cambridge, in the early 1980s, to fit as English lyrics to Theodorakis's melodies.

The conquerors, p. 47
Early drafts, Belgrade, 1989–1990; revised intermittently, Cambridge; final version, December 28, 1997.

To his daughter, mourning, p. 48
Dedicated to Jasna B. Mišić. Composed, Belgrade, 1988, and Cambridge, early 1990s.

Unmarked voices from a mass grave, p. 49
Composed in Belgrade, February 2, 1989.

This country weighs so heavy, p. 53
Dedicated to Oskar Davičo (1909–1989). Composed in Belgrade, 1987–8. Translated into Serbo-Croat by Daša Marić (*Oktobar*, No 22, Kraljevo, 1988; *Veliki školski čas*, No 20, Kragujevac, 1988; *Odzivi*, Bijelo Polje, December 1989).

The untouchables, pp. 54–55
In Memory of Primo Levi. Composed in Belgrade, 1987–8. Translated into Serbo-Croat by Daša Marić (*Oktobar*, No 22, Kraljevo, 1988) and into Macedonian by M. Čenaroski (*Razgledi*, Skopje, May 1989).

In silence: the mourner, p. 56
Composed in Belgrade, 1988, and Cambridge, early 1990s.

Wayside shrine, pp. 57–62
Dedicated to Daša Marić. Early drafts, Belgrade, November 26–27, 1988 and January 27–28, 1989. Worked on intermittently; final version, Cambridge, August 19, 1995.

Traces we cannot name, pp. 63–65
Started in Belgrade, 1987–8; repatterned in Cambridge, August 19, 1995, September 5 & 7, 1995, January 29, 1998; completed, December 17, 1998.

A TWENTIETH CENTURY DREAM, pp. 66–69
Composed in Studený, Czech Republic, November 1987, and Cambridge, December 1997 and August–September 2005.

DIAGONAL, pp. 70–72
Early drafts, Cambridge, 1984, preceding the appearance of the butterfly in Kragujevac; polished intermittently through the 1980s; completed, mid-1990s.

FLIGHT OF THE IMAGO, pp. 73–102
Imago, pl. *imagines* – entomological term: the mature, winged butterfly.

NOTHING IS LOST ALWAYS, pp. 75–76
Early drafts, Belgrade, 1989; polished intermittently, early 1990s.

THE FUTURE RECOILS, p. 77
Dedicated to Imogen Lucy Lightning (b. February 7, 2005) and Alexander Peter Lightning (b. February 22, 2006). First draft, Belgrade, November 9–10, 1988; continued, Cambridge, December 24–30, 1997; January 29, 1998; August 8, 2004; August 6–7 & 18, 2005; completed, September 22, 2005.

THE DEAD DO NOT HEAR US, pp. 78–83
Dedicated retrospectively to the memory of Martin Booth (1944–2004). *Ananke* (p. 88, and see also pp. 95 and 96): Greek goddess of Necessity. Draft first collated in Belgrade, 1988; developed, Cambridge, December 25 & 27, 1997, January 2 & 29, 1998; completed, December 17, 22 & 23, 1998.

WHAT POWER OR INTELLIGENCE, pp. 84–88
The 'Warsavian / musician' (p. 85) is Władysław Szpilman (1911–2000). See his book, *The Pianist: The Extraordinary True Story of One Man's Survival in Warsaw, 1939–1945* (Picador, 2000) and Roman Polanski's film, *The Pianist* (2002). First drafts of the poem were made in Belgrade, 1988–9; continued, Cambridge, December 23–27, 1997, October 23 & December 2–24, 1998, January 3–4, 2000, April 5, 2000, November 29, 2003, August 1–17, 2005; completed, December 25, 2005.

CONVERSATION BETWEEN A BLUE BUTTERFLY AND A MURDERED MAN AT ONE OF THE ENTRANCES TO THE UNDERWORLD, pp. 89–98
Dedicated to James Hillman. Composed in Cambridge, August 10–17, 2005, based on first notes, Belgrade, January 29, 1988.
Stjepan Filipović (p. 121), also known as Stevan, Steva and Stevo

Filipović, was born on January 27, 1916, in Opuzen, Dalmatia, and brought up in Mostar, Hercegovina. Work opportunities were better in Šumadija (central Serbia) and in 1932, aged 16, he moved to Kragujevac, where he worked as a welder in a metals factory. In 1937, he joined the Worker's Progressive Movement, a left-wing organisation, and became a party activist. He was arrested in 1939 and jailed for a year. On his release in 1940, he was banned from his workplace and joined the Communist Party. When the Nazis invaded in April 1941, he joined the Partisans in the Valjevo area, where his job was organising arms and mustering supporters. He fought in engagements at Lajkovac, Krupanj and Šabac; gained the reputation of being a fearless and astute battle leader; rose quickly through Partisan ranks; and eventually commanded his own battalion. He was captured on February 24, 1942. After four months of interrogation and torture, he was hanged publicly by the Nazis in the central square of Valjevo on June 22, 1942, aged 26. As he stood on the scaffold with the noose around his neck, he raised both hands in a defiant antifascist victory salute, and shouted, 'Long live the Communist Party. Long live the Workers' Struggle. Long live Freedom.' See the photograph (p. 121). After the war, a twelve-metre-high sculpture, based on this photo, was put up outside Kraljevo.

Filipović was made a National Hero of Yugoslavia on December 14, 1949. For an idealised biography, see Joksimović, Zoran: *Poruka ispod vesala* ['*Messages Under the Gallows*'], Dečje novine ['Children's News'] with *Savet za vaspitanje i brigu o deci, SR Srbije* ['Council for the Education and Care of Children, Socialist Republic of Serbia'], Gornji Milanovac & Belgrade, 1975. In extreme contrast, following the break-up of the Yugoslav Federation in the late 1980s and early 1990s, Croatian nationalists reclaimed him as a 'patriot' because he was anti-Serb, while some anti-Communist Serbs re-branded him as a cruel persecutor of their people.

Nature exults/in secrets, loves to hide in many veils (p. 97) – Heraclitus: 'Φύσις κρύπτεσθαι φιλεῖ' Variously translated: 'Nature loves to hide.' (Burnet, John: 'Heraclitus, Fragments', *Early Greek Philosophy*, 1892, Ch. 3); 'The real constitution of each thing is accustomed to hide itself.' (Hillman, James: *The Soul and the Underworld*, 1979); 'Things love to hide their nature' (Crowe, Malcolm: *The verses of Heraclitus of Ephesus*, 1996).

WHAT THEN IS SINGING? AND WHAT DANCING?, pp. 100–101
Dedicated to Stanley Kunitz (1905–2006). He celebrated his 100th birthday on July 29, 2005. Started in Belgrade, February and November 1988; further drafts, Cambridge, December 24–26, 1998; final version, November 29, 2003.

THINGS FALL INTO PLACE RETROSPECTIVELY, p. 102
Started in Belgrade, Autumn 1987; completed in Cambridge, 1990s.

THE BURNING BUTTERFLY, p. 105
Composed in Belgrade, 1989.

THE CORNERS OF THE MOUTH, p. 106
The title refers to Hexagram 27 of *Yijing* (*I Ching*). Composed in Belgrade, 1989; revised in Cambridge, August 2005.

WHAT SEEMED IMPOSSIBLE, p. 107
Composed in Belgrade, 1988.

SIGNET RING, p. 108
The poem describes a ring containing a black stone, on which is carved a late Roman seal. See the sketch below. The ring was loaned to me by a close friend. Written in Cambridge: first version, 1986; further drafts, December 1997, December 1998 and November 2003; final version, August 2005.

TRUE TO YOUR ABSENCE, GLORY, p. 109
To honour and remember Jacques Derrida (15 July 1930–8 October 2004). Written in Cambridge immediately following his death, October 9–10, 2004; based on first drafts, September 1 & 19, 2004.

SHALOM, p. 110
Composed in Belgrade, 1989.

GRACE, p. 111
Based on Hexagram 22 of *Yijing* (*I Ching*). Composed in Cambridge, around 1985–6.

Pronunciation of some Serbian and Croatian consonants

Spelling	Approximate English Pronunciation
c	'ts'
ć	like the palatalised 't' [*tj*] in 'tune'
č	like the 'ch' in 'church'
j	like the 'y' in 'year'
š	close to 'sh' as in 'shoe'
ž	close to the 's' in 'fusion'

Some Serbian and Croatian words and names in this book

crkva	church
čas	class, lesson
Četnik, pl. *Četnici*	Anglicised to 'Chetnik'; etym. *četa*, troop, band; named after the armed irregulars who harassed the Turks in the 19th century. (1) trooper, in the First World War. (2) member of Serbian nationalist and royalist troop or band in the Second World War, mainly under leadership of Colonel Dragoljub (Draža) Mihajlović, otherwise known as the *Ravna Gora* group. (3) pejor. Serb nationalist.
crven (f. -*a*)	red
dan	day
držim	I hold, I'm holding
duša (pl. -*e*)	soul
gimnazija	grammar school, *lycée*
gora	mountain, hill, high place
gornji	higher
kraguj	hawk, sparrowhawk
Kragujevac	etym. 'Hawk's Town'
kletva	curse
književnost	literature
komanda	corps, command (military)
kralj	king
Kraljevo	etym. 'King's Town'
	Krvava bajka 'Bloody Fable/Fairy Tale', title of poem by Desanka Maksimović about the Šumarice massacre, written two days after it.
Ljotićevci	followers of Dimitrije V. Ljotić. See *Srpski Dobrovoljački Odred* and *ZBOR* below.

mladost	youth
moj (f. *–a*)	my
nada	hope
naš (f. *–a*)	our
Nemojte	Don't (plural)
odred	detachment (military)
polje	field
Pucajte	Shoot! (plural)
Prva muška gimnazija	'First Boys' Grammar School'
rad	work
ravan (f. *ravna*)	flat, level
sada	now
srce	heart
star (f. *–a*)	old
Stara crkva	old church
Srpski dobrovoljački odred	'Serbian Volunteer Detachment'; later, the *Srpska dobrovoljačka komanda* or *Serbische Freiwilligenkorps* ['Serbian Volunteer Corps']: uniformed military wing of the Serbian collaborationist organisation *ZBOR* (q.v.), led by Dimitrije V. Ljotić. Its members took active part in the round-up and selection of civilians before the Kragujevac massacre. See also *Ljotićevci*.
šuma	forest, wood
Šumadija	Part of central Serbia; etym. *šuma*.
Šumarice	'Spinneys', 'little wooded areas'; site of the 1941 massacre outside Kragujevac; etym. *šuma*.
Veliki školski čas	'The Big School Lesson', 'The Great Lesson': title of event commemorating the Šumarice massacre, since 1962, held annually at the memorial site on 21 October. The title refers to the deaths of pupils and their teachers.
Vojno tehnički zavod	'Military Technical Bureau'
zastava	banner, flag
ZBOR	(1) lit. 'assembly, rally, gathering, meeting'. (2) name of the 'Yugoslav People's Movement', founded 1935, under the leadership of Dimitrije V. Ljotić. (3) Also intended as acronym: *Združena borbena organizacija rada* ['United Combat Work Organisation']. (4) Serbian

Fascist organisation that collaborated with Nazis in World War II. See *Srpska dobrovoljačka odred*. Its members were also called *Ljotićevci* ('followers of Ljotić' : q. v.).

Živima 'For the living'.

RB
CAMBRIDGE
APRIL 27, 2006, JULY 8, 2008 & MAY 17, 2011

151

Lightning Source UK Ltd.
Milton Keynes UK
UKOW04f1840230215

246766UK00001B/1/P